Authentic.
Creative.
Innovative.

Praise for the Trencherman's Guide

'A must-have guide for anyone who loves great food'

Paul Ainsworth

'The only independent, quality-controlled guide in the South West'

Michael Caines MBE

'A guide with teeth'

Rick Stein CBE

'It holds a special position in promoting excellence'

Jack Stein

'Very few areas of the country have a guide like Trencherman's, which rivals Hardens or Michelin'

William Sitwell

edition
33

PARTNERS

CLASSIC
—— FINE FOODS ——

The CORNISH
FISHMONGER
From WING of St MAWES Ltd.

HALLGARTEN
& NOVUM WINES

HARVEY & BROCKLESS
the fine food co

NAVAS
PREMIUM BOTANICAL MIXERS

EST · 1851
ST AUSTELL
BREWERY

St.Ewe
Delicious Free Range Eggs

TREVETHAN
SINCE 1929

Editor
Abi Manning

Editorial team
Ting Baker
Alice Humphrys
Melissa Morris
Jane Rakison
Rosanna Rothery
Lucy Shrimpton
Selena Young

Editorial director
Jo Rees

Design
Christopher Mulholland

Commercial
Claire Fegan
Jeni Smith

Publishing
Charlotte Cummins
Tamsin Powell

Managing director
Nick Cooper

Published by Salt Media
ideas@saltmedia.co.uk
01271 859299
saltmedia.co.uk

We're serious about protecting the planet which is why
we print using solvent-free inks on FSC® certified paper,
working with a printer that holds ISO14001 certification for
environmental good practice.

'A kaleidoscopic array of dining concepts'

From the editor

There was once a clear distinction between fine dining and casual eats, but that line has become increasingly blurred in recent years.

Previously, "fine dining" establishments were easily identified by their formal dress code, starched tablecloths, classical cooking and sommelier. But diners' tastes have evolved.

It's no bad thing. Now, a kaleidoscopic array of dining concepts exists within the world of high-end hospitality. In the following pages, you'll discover establishments that remain bastions of tradition, alongside those revelling in ultra-modern minimalism, farm-to-fork rusticity, international flavours and more.

This broad canvas also enables restaurants to be flexible with their offering. We've recently seen some small-plates venues pivot to trad à la carte, and tasting-menu-only spots offering shorter set menus, while other restaurants have widened their reach through brewery collabs and food festivals.

Another trend is the rise of flame and feasting experiences. There's something primal in gathering with like-minded diners amid the elements while bonding over good food. This back-to-nature, relationship-led approach aligns with chefs using hyper-local produce where connections with growers, farmers and fishermen* run deeper than simply a business relationship.

Regardless of vibe, dress code or the presence of a dessert trolley, the thread that runs through every Trencherman's member restaurant – whether old-school or ultra-casual – is quality. Each holds the same high standards in delivering a truly exceptional guest experience.

Here's to some delicious adventures in the South West. Let me know where you've enjoyed visiting.

Abi Manning
Editor
⊙ abi_manning_

*The term 'fishermen' is used throughout the guide and includes men and women in the catching sector. The term is widely accepted in the industry as a respected occupational identity rather than a gendered label. (Info: UK Women in Fisheries)

Contents

About the guide

Since the *Trencherman's Guide* was established in 1992, it has built a rock-solid reputation as the gourmet's definitive passport to the most exquisite dining experiences in the South West.

Rick Stein describes it as *'a guide with teeth'* due to the strict entry criteria that restaurants must meet in order to be included.

Establishments are invited to be a member based on reaching a number of points in an extremely stringent scoring system. Points are accumulated based on inclusion in a select list of renowned national guides or scoring by our in-house team of experienced food journalists. They visit venues throughout the year and complete detailed reports with criteria such as food, presentation, drinks, setting and service.

Extra-special dining experiences

When a restaurant achieves an exceptionally high score, it's categorised as a "higher member". These establishments combine cooking of the highest order with polished service, delivered in a setting that's an exceptional example of its type – from impeccable dining pubs to grand manor houses and edge-of-the-water restaurants. Similarly, the wine list and other drinks provisions will be especially interesting, unusual or sizeable. Expect to find many wines by the glass, a breadth of local spirits and creative cocktails.

Authentic knowledge

One distinct feature that sets the *Trencherman's Guide* apart from other dining guides is the authentic knowledge of the team behind it. They all live in the South West and have their fingers on the pulse of the region's dining scene, enjoying relationships with its hospitality industry that span decades. They also produce sister South West publications *Food Lifestyle* magazine and the *Indy Coffee Guides*.

In addition, the guide is overseen by a committee of industry experts (pictured right), chaired by Michelin-star-holding chef Michael Caines MBE.

Trencherman's Awards

Each year, the best of the best of South West hospitality come together at the prestigious Trencherman's Awards, which are voted for by our readers.

Check out what happened at the 2025 awards by flicking to page 16.

The ***Trencherman's Guide*** is overseen by a committee of industry experts. **Clockwise from top left:** Abi Manning, editor of the *Trencherman's Guide*; Jo Rees and Nick Cooper, co-founders of Salt Media; Veryan Palmer, hotelier; Michael Caines MBE, chef and restaurateur (committee chairman).

Behind the scenes at the Trencherman's Awards 2025

Following thousands of votes, the winners of the Trencherman's Awards 2025 were revealed at a glamorous soirée at Homewood near Bath

Photographs by Guy Harrop

For the Trencherman's Awards 2025, we headed to Homewood, the luxuriously eclectic, grand Georgian house just outside Bath, for a fabulous ceremony and multi-course supper on March 24. Attendees included the movers and shakers of the South West dining scene: celebrated chefs, restaurateurs, hoteliers, and leading food and drinks businesses.

A champagne reception and no-dig garden canapés from Homewood were followed by a supper prepared by some of last year's winners, along with the host chef.

Left to right: Nicholas Balfe, Ben Palmer, Jamie Forman, Ayesha Kalaji

Ben Palmer (Best Trencherman's Chef 2024) of The Sardine Factory, Looe, cooked his *Great British Menu*-winning golden beetroot dish, Firefly, for the starter.

This was followed by a fish course of gin-cured trout with no-dig garden pickles, fennel and balsamic by Jamie Forman of Homewood.

The main course was cooked by Nicholas Balfe of Holm in South Petherton (Best Trencherman's Restaurant 2024) and comprised Otter Valley cull yaw with anchovy, potato and wild garlic.

Dessert of dark chocolate and Persian lime crémeux with lime and Arak sorbet, finger limes, praline paillette feuilletine, hazelnut and chocolate tuile was prepared by

Ayesha Kalaji of Queen of Cups in Glastonbury (Best Trencherman's Newcomer 2024). Ayesha switched from kitchen to stage soon after guests finished dessert as she was announced Best Chef 2025 at the end of the evening.

Turn the page to see who won and what went down on the night.

Award for Special Contribution

Sponsored by Trevethan Distillery

Winner
Paul Ainsworth

Best Trencherman's Chef

Sponsored by Hallgarten & Novum Wines

Winner
Ayesha Kalaji of The Queen of Cups, Glastonbury

Finalists
Paul Ainsworth of Paul Ainsworth at No6, Padstow
Isabel Joscelyne of Prawn on the Lawn, Padstow
Merlin Labron-Johnson of Osip, Bruton
Tommy Thorn of Puro, Clevedon

Best Trencherman's Restaurant

Sponsored by Alliance

Winner
Barnaby's, Padstow

Finalists
BANK, Bristol
The Clockspire, Sherborne
Osip, Bruton
Paul Ainsworth at No6, Padstow

Best Trencherman's Hotel

Sponsored by Classic Fine Foods

Winner
St Michaels Resort, Falmouth

Finalists
Bovey Castle, Dartmoor
The Headland Hotel, Newquay
Hotel Endsleigh, Dartmoor
The Priory Hotel, Wareham

Best Trencherman's Pub
Sponsored by Sharp's Brewing Co

Winner
The Chagford Inn, Dartmoor

Finalists
Bearslake Inn, Dartmoor
Chequers, Bath
The Gurnard's Head, Zennor
The Tartan Fox, Newquay

Award for Creativity and Innovation
Sponsored by St. Ewe

Winner
Osip, Bruton

Finalists
Àclèaf, near Plymouth
Ardor, St Ives
Ogo at Bedruthan, Mawgan Porth
Reef Knot Restaurant at The Idle Rocks, St Mawes

Best Front of House Team
Sponsored by Navas

Winner
The Clockspire, Sherborne

Finalists
Beach House Falmouth (formerly Hooked on the Rocks)
The Farm Table, Topsham
Iford Manor Kitchen, near Bath
Salumi Bar & Eatery, Plymouth

Best Trencherman's Newcomer

Sponsored by Harvey & Brockless

Winner
Iford Manor Kitchen, near Bath

Finalists
Barnaby's, Padstow
The Chagford Inn, Dartmoor
The Farm Table, Topsham
Hotel Tresanton, St Mawes

Best Bar List

Sponsored by South West 660

Winner
The Farm Table, Topsham

Finalists
Bovey Castle, Dartmoor
Corkage, Bath
Hive Beach Cafe, Burton Bradstock
Roth Bar, Bruton

Special thanks

The Trencherman's Awards 2025 were supported by Alliance, Churchill China, Classic Fine Foods, Flying Fish Seafoods, Hallgarten & Novum Wines, Harvey & Brockless, Navas, Otter Valley Farms, Sharp's Brewing Co, St. Ewe, and Trevethan Distillery.

More ways to discover exceptional restaurants

Trencherman's online

The Trencherman's website has had a major glow-up. Enter exclusive competitions with exceptional dine and stay prizes, search for restaurants in the region, discover inspiring curations and get the dates and details of dining events.

trenchermans-guide.com

Receive the Trencherman's newsletter

Newsletter subscribers are the first to hear about incredible competitions, events, hot-off-the-press news, features and more.

They also receive advance notification of voting for the annual Trencherman's Awards.

Head to the Trencherman's website to sign up.

Be social

Join our online community and follow the team's dining adventures across the South West via the Trencherman's social channels.

⊙ **trenchermans_guide**

f **The Trencherman's Guide**

How to use the guide

To make the guide easy to use, the restaurants are grouped by geographical region.

You'll find each venue plotted on a map at the beginning of each section, with a map number that's mirrored on each profile page. Alternatively, look up names you know in the index in the back of the book.

What the symbols mean

Restaurants that have achieved an exceptionally high Trencherman's score

Restaurants where you can also stay the night

Cornwall

Cornwall

Numbers on the map correspond to the numbers next to the restaurants in the guide.

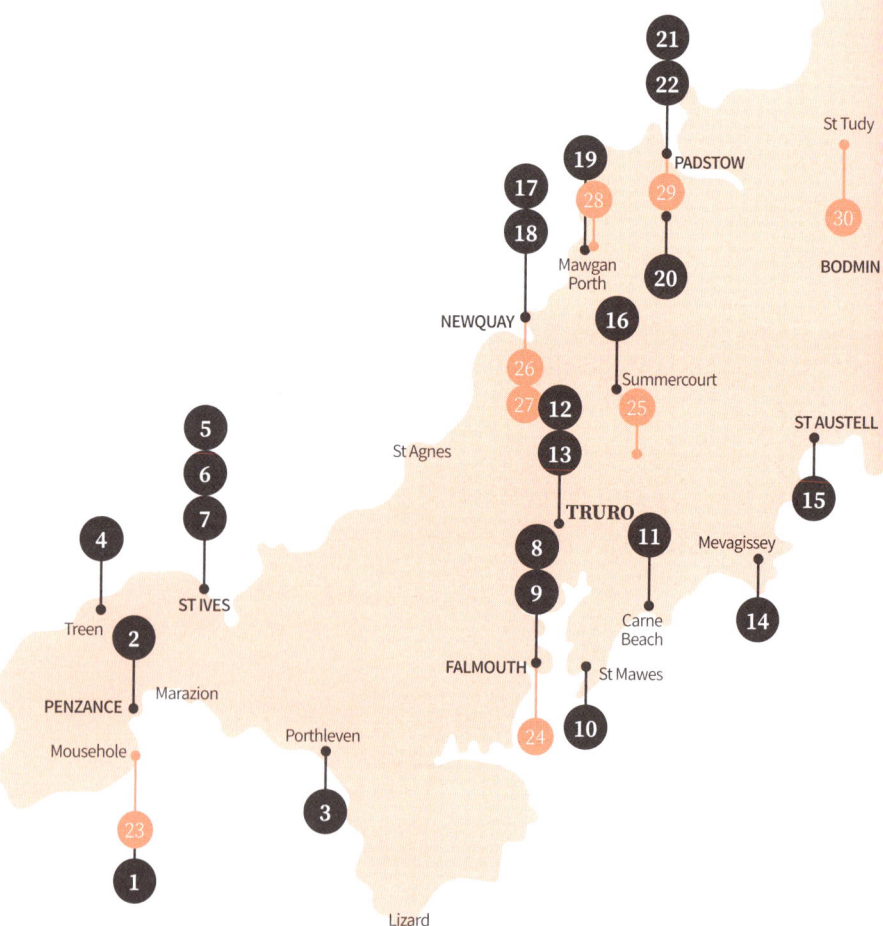

Dartmoor National Park

LOOE

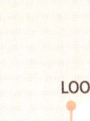

Locations are approximate

1 The Old Coastguard

Creative outpost on a clifftop

Part of Charles and Edmund Inkin's EATDRINKSLEEP stable (sister venues include chef fave The Gurnard's Head near Zennor and The Felin Fach Griffin in Wales), this restaurant with rooms resides in the beautiful fishing village of Mousehole.

Its menu is dictated by what's local and in season. Newlyn's dayboats tie up a mere two miles west, so fish is a given, but head chef Danny Garland also pays homage to the superb meats, cheeses and veg produced nearby. His culinary background (he previously cooked with Yotam Ottolenghi) also inspires creative plant-based and vegetarian compilations.

Choose from three charming places to wine and dine: the scrubbed wooden tables of the Upper Deck with their views to St Clement's Isle; the comfy sofas on the Sun Deck overlooking the palm-lined garden; or, best of all, on the terrace with its ocean panorama.

The menu may be rooted in traditional brasserie-style cooking, but when ingredients this good are treated with care dishes are elevated above the norm. Stuffed courgette flower, for example, comprises lobster, lime leaf and roasted-chilli jam, while brown crab is paired with handmade stracci pasta, heritage tomatoes and samphire.

Many of the cosy bedrooms feature views across Mount's Bay and out to sea, so staying the night is seriously tempting.

Trencherman's tip

During the summer, make a beeline for The Crab Shack in the garden. Here, seafood and lighter snacks are served all day alongside drinks such as craft beer and locally roasted speciality coffee from Yallah.

Chef **Danny Garland** | 3-course dinner from **£48** | Seats **100** | Bedrooms **14** | Room rate from **£182.50** | **EV charging**
oldcoastguardhotel.co.uk | The Parade, Mousehole, Penzance, Cornwall, TR19 6PR | **01736 731222**

2 The Tolcarne Inn

Location, location, location

Sat beside the working harbour at Newlyn, The Tolcarne Inn is just steps from one of the UK's most prolific fishing ports. Chef-owner Ben Tunnicliffe (formerly of Michelin-starred The Abbey in Penzance) harnesses this bounty with a menu that constantly shifts to reflect the freshest catch.

A large chalkboard menu showcases bold, intuitive cooking that celebrates simplicity and depth of flavour. Think red mullet with lemon-glazed salsify and fennel, ray wing with smoked-ham croquettes and cider mustard, or weaver fish served with scallop-roe taramasalata and cucumber chutney. There's nothing fussy here, just honest, flavour-driven plates grounded in Cornish produce.

Everything is made in-house, from sauces and stocks to desserts. The drinks offering is equally well considered, with local ales, ciders and a wine list carefully curated to complement the seafood-led dishes.

Trencherman's tip

The inn dates back to 1717. While it doesn't lean into a historical-memorabilia aesthetic, the sense of heritage is felt in the building's thick stone walls, timber beams and cosy wood burner. The relaxed space puts the focus firmly on what's on the plate (and in the glass).

Chef **Ben Tunnicliffe** | 3-course dinner from **£53** | Seats **35**
tolcarneinn.co.uk | Newlyn, Penzance, Cornwall, TR18 5PR | 01736 363074

3 Kota Food & Wine

Porthleven pintxos with Asian zing

Kota, by *Great British Menu* veteran Jude Kereama, has entered its relaxed yet refined era following a restaurant glow-up and redefined dining concept.

In this new chapter, the restaurant retains its status as the go-to spot for three-AA-rosette dining in Porthleven, but now features a flexible menu. Guests choose from a line-up of snacks, Cornish pintxos, daily specials and a chef's menu: six courses from the menu, served tasting-menu style.

The dishes are skilfully executed by Jude's good friend and head chef Ross Sloan. Standouts from the updated offering include Falmouth Bay oysters (try them crispy potato-wrapped and topped with tonbori furikake), crab tortilla okonomiyaki, and gurnard with bouillabaisse, sabayon, rouille and black olive caramel.

Menus are utterly produce-led, with emphasis placed on supporting Kota's local suppliers.

A brand new bar is designed for guests to pop in and stay a while, enjoying the extensive wine list, snappy cocktails (the wakame seaweed vodka martini is highly recommended) and Cornish beers from Sharp's.

Trencherman's tip

Book one of the three harbour-view bedrooms above the restaurant to take full advantage of the regularly changing wine list. After a good night's sleep, swing by sister bar and kitchen Kota Kai for laid-back lunching.

Chef **Ross Sloan** | 4-course dinner from **£52.50** | Seats **36** | Bedrooms **3** | Room rate from **£120**
kotarestaurant.co.uk | Harbour Head, Porthleven, Helston, Cornwall, TR13 9JA | **01326 562407**

4 The Gurnard's Head

Arty and authentic

Perched in a secluded spot on Penwith moorland just a few miles from St Ives, this relaxed and rustic dining pub with rooms is the epitome of Cornish comfort.

Owned and stewarded by brothers Charles and Edmund Inkin (proprietors of The Old Coastguard in Mousehole and The Felin Fach Griffin in Wales), the iconic bright yellow inn overlooking the Atlantic is comfortable and well appointed. However, it's the food and warm hospitality that make it truly memorable.

Boldness runs throughout – from the buttery colour of the exterior and dining rooms to the ever-evolving menu. Long-time head chef Max Wilson crafts dishes from whatever seasonal ingredients arrive on his doorstep, including dayboat-delivered seafood, locally reared meats and farm-fresh veg.

Standout dishes include whole plaice served with caper, shallot, almond and lemon butter; ribeye steak with green beans, stilton, gherkin and caper salad and beef-dripping hash brown; and half-shell scallops served simply with garlic butter, chives and lemon.

To complement this good cooking, the pub features an exceptional – and eclectic – wine list, which includes finds from new and little-known winemakers and a number of UK wineries. Twenty wines by the glass and carafe make pairing with each course a breeze.

Trencherman's tip

If the weather's good, opt for a pint of Verdant Cornish craft beer at the outside bar, The Cow Shed. Peckish? A casual all-day menu – including gourmet burgers – is available for those arriving between meals.

Chef **Max Wilson** | 3-course dinner from **£48** | Seats **60** | Bedrooms **8** | Room rate from **£167.50**
gurnardshead.co.uk | Zennor, St Ives, Cornwall, TR26 3DE | **01736 796928**

5 Ardor

Mediterranean hospitality

In the heart of the popular seaside town of St Ives, with its mosaic of turquoise sea, cobbled streets and indie shops, is vibrant Ardor, which specialises in the culinary traditions of the Iberian Peninsula. Rich, earthy tones and hand-painted Moroccan tiles hint at chef-patron Dorian Janmaat's love of authentic Mediterranean cooking.

The chef's dedication to simplicity, flavour and fresh Cornish produce can be savoured in everything from Spanish-inspired pintxos and tapas to dry-aged cuts, rotisserie chicken and seafood dishes.

Start the Mediterranean odyssey with freshly shucked oysters followed by fried aubergine with honey and olive – the latter an artful balance of sweet, salty and umami flavours.

Mains include the likes of monkfish and prawn skewer – the juicy, plump hunks of seafood elevated by the addition of a piquant Canarian sauce. Heartier sharing options include dry-aged sirloin on the bone, cooked over charcoal and served with a rich garlic butter. Or, for a Med-inspired centrepiece, opt for the sharing paella of ultra-fresh fish and charred piparra peppers.

Desserts lean into Spanish tradition, with classics including gooey basque cheesecake and silky crema catalana with a caramelised top.

Ardor epitomises the essence of Mediterranean hospitality: a warm atmosphere, sharing dishes and a curated list of southern European wines and crafted cocktails.

Trencherman's tip

Sit downstairs where an open kitchen and chefs' counter offer front-row seats to the culinary action.

Chef **Dorian Janmaat** | 3-course dinner from **£45** | Seats **65**
ardorstives.co.uk | 45 Fore Street, St Ives, Cornwall, TR26 1HE | **01736 794004**

6 Porthminster Beach Cafe

Seafood artistry and a sensational seascape

This restaurant, perched on the white sands of Porthminster Beach, delivers seafood and a seascape whose beauty rivals that of the art hanging in nearby Tate St Ives.

Many restaurants in coastal destinations close their shutters in the winter months, but this perennially popular (and multi-award-winning) spot bustles regardless of the season.

Vibrant dishes stream from the kitchen, landing on tables in the pared-back dining room where they are swiftly devoured. On balmy days, diners flock to the outdoor terrace to dine with the salty breeze brushing their skin.

The restaurant enjoys great prestige thanks to head chef Ben Prior (formerly of Ben's Cornish Kitchen in Marazion) and chef-owner Mick Smith's sterling reputation for Asian- and Mediterranean-inspired cooking.

The chefs craft dishes based on the bounty of produce at their fingertips. Expect the freshest seafood, foraged coastal ingredients and garden-grown herbs and veg.

Menus are switched up regularly, but a typical Porthminster supper could include such beauties as hand-dived scallops, whole roast turbot to share, and black spice squid with citrus miso. Sunday roasts are available in autumn and winter.

Leave room for inventive pudding combos like mango and marshmallow with thai-curry sorbet.

Trencherman's tip

Getting hitched? Porthminster Beach Cafe is a popular (and picturesque) venue for a wedding reception or other special occasions.

Chef **Ben Prior** | 3-course dinner from £**50** | Seats **82**

porthminstercafe.co.uk | Porthminster Beach, St Ives, Cornwall, TR26 2EB | **01736 795352**

![Restaurant interior with round tables, plush chairs, pendant lighting, and floor-to-ceiling windows overlooking the sea]

7 Walter's on The Beach at Carbis Bay Estate

Dark glamour at the seaside

It's hard to beat the drama of dinner at Walter's on The Beach at Carbis Bay Hotel & Estate. Step out of the bright seascape of the beachside terrace and cross the threshold into a space where you're cloaked in soft lighting and luxury. This is a venue that allows you to blend into the background and let your hair down.

From its funky soundtrack and gleaming cocktail bar to a menu crammed with culinary surprises, everything at Walter's screams *'let the good times roll'*.

Exec chef Andrew Houghton has created a menu of well-executed, internationally inspired dishes, which includes intriguing options for those who like to inject a little je ne sais quoi into their dining experience.

Experience his penchant for delivering the unexpected in dishes such as a starter of fresh lobster sandwiched in a giant macaron – an intriguing yet successful pairing of the French confection with the briny sweetness of shellfish.

Mains provide further cultural mash-ups. Try the light and delicate flavours of ChalkStream trout paired with the Japanese notes of umami-rich bonita sauce, encased in the puff pastry of a British wellington.

Carbis Bay Hotel & Estate offers an array of accommodation so you can turn dinner into a full gourmet getaway. The most spectacular are its lodges, built artfully into the hillside and with direct access to the privately owned beach.

Trencherman's tip

Before sitting down to dine, don't miss the theatrical experience of perching at the bar and watching mixologist Ionut Ghiba craft some of the best cocktails outside London.

Chef **Andrew Houghton** | 3-course dinner from **£85** | Seats **40** | Bedrooms **68** | Room rate from **£250** | **EV charging**
carbisbayhotel.co.uk | Carbis Bay Estate, St Ives, Cornwall, TR26 2NP | **01736 795311**

8 Indidog Harbourside Restaurant

Feelgood feasting

This buzzy restaurant, with its huge windows and terrace overlooking the glassy waters of Falmouth Harbour, delivers city vibes at the seaside.

Grab a table in the large space and revel in the theatre of an open kitchen and the bustle of a well-run restaurant in full swing. Or bag a waterside spot outdoors for sunny dining with the scent of the ocean on the breeze.

Head chef Alfred Hazlitt's cooking complements this feelgood setting. His lunch and dinner menus are modern British in style, elegantly executed and forged from uber-local ingredients that include luscious salads grown at Soul Farm on the Trefusis Estate.

The local Mylor scallops – served in the half shell with green-chilli jam, apple, lemon and daikon – are a fabulous way to start. Or order the knockout smoked cod's roe served with lacy sourdough crisps.

Follow with dishes such as miso-glazed monkfish in an umami broth with sautéed napa cabbage, coriander and radish, and finish with English strawberries served three ways with earl grey ice cream and pink-peppercorn meringue.

Trencherman's tip

Indidog's generous size makes it a great spot to gather with a crowd for sundowners and celebrations – without stinting on the quality of the food.

Chef **Alfred Hazlitt** | 3-course dinner from **£35** | Seats **100**
indidogeatery.com | 28a Market Street, Falmouth, Cornwall, TR11 3AT | 01326 450699

9 The Greenbank Hotel

Historic hotel with panoramic views

Falmouth may have been home to many hotels of note, but none have stood the test of time like The Greenbank. Dating to 1640, the building overlooking the Fal Estuary has hosted many illustrious guests including *The Wind in the Willows* **author Kenneth Grahame.**

While the hotel is steeped in history, the atmosphere is casual and contemporary. At the Water's Edge restaurant, creative dishes showcasing the finest Cornish ingredients are concocted by head chef Bobby Southworth and executive chef Nick Hodges. Expect gems such as pan-seared scallops with pork belly, black pudding, preserved peach and endive. Balmy day? The terrace is a glorious alfresco dining spot.

After dinner, settle at the adjoining Water's Edge bar to watch the boats on the harbour (the hotel has its own private pontoon) while indulging in a creative cocktail. For an alternative dining destination, head below deck to The Working Boat pub to sink a local craft beer and enjoy hearty pub fare.

The restaurant hosts superb foodie events such as Bobby's Taste of Cornwall and a Friday cocktail club.

Make it a full gourmet getaway by booking one of the contemporary bedrooms. They're an excellent base from which to explore the nearby National Maritime Museum Cornwall, Pendennis Castle and the South West Coast Path.

Trencherman's tip

Check out sister hotels The Alverton in Truro and The Falmouth for traditional luxury with modern comforts.

Chef **Bobby Southworth** | 3-course dinner from **£45** | Seats **70** | Bedrooms **61** | Room rate from **£129** | **EV charging**
greenbank-hotel.co.uk | Harbourside, Falmouth, Cornwall, TR11 2SR | **01326 312440**

10 Reef Knot Restaurant at The Idle Rocks

Uber-fresh sustainable seafood

Whether you're watching the sun set over the water, sipping cocktails on the harbour-view terrace, dining on the daily catch in the Reef Knot Restaurant or reviving in the SEVAN Spa, The Idle Rocks guarantees a feast of indulgences.

The Relais & Châteaux hotel's waterfront location and exemplary hospitality are reason enough to visit, but in-the-know foodies flock for the inventive piscatorial offering from head chef Carla Jones and team.

The talented chef's menu majors on sustainably caught Cornish fish paired with the finest seasonal and local produce. Ingredients are sourced through carefully developed relationships with suppliers. The restaurant even has its own dedicated St Mawes fisherman, Gareth Austin, who daily delivers ultra-fresh seafood from local waters.

Signature dishes include Cornish octopus with fennel and blood orange, Cornish cod with kohlrabi, brown shrimp, apple, cucumber and beurre noisette, and curried monkfish with soy, lime, avocado and sesame granola.

The Michelin Key-rated rooms feature a contemporary coastal style, making this a brilliant base from which to explore the Roseland peninsula. Book a Grand Seaview Room for the opportunity to soak in a window-side tub while watching boats glide across the bay.

Trencherman's tip

On Saturday lunchtimes in summer, the terrace comes alive with a celebratory mash-up of Cornish seafood, rosé and sunshine, as guests enjoy the daily local catch paired with iconic wines from Château d'Esclans.

Chef **Carla Jones** | 3-course dinner from **£85** | Seats **50** | Bedrooms **18** | Room rate from **£265** | **EV charging**
idlerocks.com | Harbourside, St Mawes, Cornwall, TR2 5AN | 01326 270270

Elevate your spirit

navasdrinks.com

Blended with Cornish spring water
Partnered with the Eden Project
Certified B Corp

NAVAS
PREMIUM BOTANICAL MIXERS

11 The Quarterdeck Seafood Restaurant at The Nare

Old-school hospitality by the sea

The Nare is one of an increasingly rare breed of uber-traditional hotels. In a sector leaning into pared-back minimalism, small plates and casual vibes, it has proudly nailed its colours to the mast as a luxurious old-school hotel that does formality with buckets of charm.

Sea-inspired synergy pervades every part of the experience, thanks to the hotel's location above beautiful Carne Beach. Whether you're sipping a sherry on a sea-view balcony, swimming lengths of the ocean-facing outdoor pool, or melting away in the beach-house hot tub facing the rugged headland, views are maximised at every turn.

The ocean connection continues in the yacht-themed Quarterdeck Seafood Restaurant. Its menu is a celebration of the bountiful south coast. A starter of St Mawes octopus comprises a curled tentacle on a bed of corn velouté with a jalapeño and passionfruit glaze, crunchy quinoa tuile and chimichurri. The marine theme is even lent to dishes more traditionally rooted in the land. A meaty monkfish wellington, encased in prawn mousse and accompanied by a potato terrine and heritage carrots, is zapped with curried warmth courtesy of cumin and vadouvan.

Proprietor Toby Ashworth's love of wine is evident in an extensive cellar that's a treasure trove of exceptional bottles from across the globe, as well as a few from local vineyards.

Trencherman's tip

The Nare's other restaurant, The Dining Room, is the spot for traditional five-course table d'hôte dining. Classic silver service, a daily changing menu, an hors d'oeuvres trolley and gueridon-served flambés bring theatre and a sense of occasion – reflected in guests' attire of jackets and ties and fancy frocks.

Chef **Andre Lima** | 3-course dinner from **£60** | Seats **60** | Bedrooms **40** | Room rate from **£406** | **EV charging**
narehotel.co.uk | Carne Beach, Veryan-in-Roseland, Cornwall, TR2 5PF | **01872 501111**

12 Petty Fours

Stimulating dinner spot

Pint-size Petty Fours, with its 20 covers and out-of-the-way location, is somewhat hidden in Cornwall's capital of Truro. Take this as your heads-up that seeking it out is absolutely worth the effort.

Chef-patron Alfred Petty (hence the restaurant's name) crafts refined dishes in two- or three-course set menus and an eight-course tasting menu.

As one might expect at such a bijou restaurant, the menu is limited – a good thing as it reveals everything to be crafted from scratch. Naturally, each menu includes petits fours, as well as amuse bouche like crisp cornets of chicken liver parfait with chilli jam sweetness.

Careful attention to detail is seen in starters such as an elegant curation of pink, yellow and purple beetroots, which are roasted, pared and

pickled before being artfully arranged with pear, fig, walnuts and fresh leaves, then drizzled with peppery green olive oil.

Mains include the likes of short-rib tortellini, where the umami richness of a beef broth is punctuated by the addition of pickled mushrooms. Confections such as elegant lemon meringue pie with impeccable honeycomb decoration end a meal in style.

Trencherman's tip

Once the last chocolate truffle has been devoured, guests can stretch the evening's pleasures into the next morning thanks to a parting gift of homemade granola.

Chef **Alfred Petty** | 3-course dinner from **£48** | Seats **20**
pettyfours.co.uk | 4-5 Old Bridge Street, Truro, Cornwall, TR1 2AQ | 07354 427160

13 The Alverton Hotel

City escapism

A hidden treasure in the city of Truro, The Alverton (sister to The Greenbank and The Falmouth hotels) is tucked away at the top of a winding drive and surrounded by mature gardens. It feels a world away from the bustle of the city, despite being just a ten-minute stroll from its centre.

The Grade II*-listed hotel's riches are revealed at every turn: on discovering its history as a private residence and convent; when unwinding on the sunny terrace, cocktail in hand; and on snoozing in one of the luxurious bedrooms or suites.

The true jewel, however, is the two-AA-rosette cooking from a skilled team led by head chef Ollie Wyatt and executive chef Nick Hodges. The à la carte menu is flush with Cornish fare from land and sea, including Ollie's pick of the local dayboat catch.

Dishes such as Kilhallon Farm beef fillet with roasted cauliflower purée, Davidstow rarebit, leek, gherkin and red wine jus rub shoulders with fresh-egg tagliatelle with mussels, clams, samphire and chilli, and ravioli of caramelised pear and goat's cheese with spinach and sage butter.

Foraged accompaniments elevate seasonal flavours to centre stage in the likes of chocolate tart with seasonal berries.

Trencherman's tip

Keenly priced weekly specials include Fizz and Chip Fridays and Thursday Cocktail Club, while seasonal events include Lobster on the Lawn and Ollie's Taste of Truro.

Chef **Ollie Wyatt** | 3-course dinner from **£45** | Seats **70** | Bedrooms **53** | Room rate from **£119** | **EV charging**
thealverton.co.uk | Tregolls Road, Truro, Cornwall, TR1 1ZQ | 01872 276633

14 The Barley Sheaf at Gorran

Country pub celebrating Cornwall

The MO of this attractive Grade II-listed pub is to celebrate all things Cornish. Browse the menus from chef-director Daniel Hyams to discover ingredients foraged, sourced, reared and grown nearby – including in the pub's garden.

It's all part of the vision to create the perfect community pub, and one the team would love to encounter themselves.

Daniel took over The Barley Sheaf in 2024, and is building a reputation for crafting deliciously well-executed dishes that reflect the surrounding seascape and countryside.

He has cooked in kitchens across the globe, including various Michelin-starred establishments, and this experience shines through in classic pub dishes, and tasting and à la carte menus. To revel in uber seasonal

produce, try From the Garden – a dish packed with the day's pub-garden pickings (grown and harvested by the chef).

Fish from nearby Mevagissey and Gorran Haven harbours provide the dayboat catch of the day.

The pub's much-loved scotch egg has been on the menu since day one and, in its present incarnation, comprises a St Ewe Dippy Scotch Egg with a blue-cheese soldier and miso mayo.

Trencherman's tip

Balmy day? Pick something good from the extensive wine list or line-up of local beers and sip in the garden.

Chef **Daniel Hyams** | 3-course dinner from **£48** | Seats **60**

thebarleysheafgorran.co.uk | Gorran Churchtown, St Austell, Cornwall, PL26 6HN | 01726 843330

15 Edie's

Family finesse

Edie's, in the coastal resort of Carlyon Bay near St Austell, is a thoroughly family affair. Cornishman Nigel Brown heads up the kitchen, his wife Kelly runs front of house and their eponymous daughter Edie creates mixology magic behind the bar.

Together the trio have created a dining experience of note. It's no wonder, really, since Nigel spent 20 years cheffing with culinary luminaries such as Raymond Blanc at Le Petit Blanc (where Kelly also worked) and Bill Granger in Sydney, before bringing his well-honed skills home.

Guests can take a pew in the raised seating area overlooking the open kitchen to watch as Nigel transforms local ingredients into flavourful combinations. The result is unfussy modern British dishes that reflect his French training.

Fresh fish is prominent on the seasonal menu, with piscatorial pleasures including combinations like Cornish fish soup with rouille, crab and apple salad, and Cornish hake with sauté potatoes, wilted baby gem and shellfish vermouth cream.

Pair the good food with wines from a global list, while beers, gins and vodkas in the well-stocked bar are exclusively Cornish.

Kelly has a wealth of experience in managing high-profile restaurants and delivers warm, efficient service. The decor is relaxed with whitewashed brick walls, eclectic art and cookbook-stacked shelves.

Trencherman's tip

Northern soul and old-school funk provide a soundtrack in pleasing counterpoint to the contemporary dining experience.

Chef **Nigel Brown** | 3-course dinner from **£35** | Seats **42**
edies.restaurant | 10 Beach Road, Carlyon Bay, St Austell, Cornwall, PL25 3PH | **01726 813888**

![photograph of two chefs standing in front of a stone pub building with "The Tartan Fox by Adam Handling" sign]

16 The Tartan Fox by Adam Handling

No-waste feasting in a country pub

Great British Menu-winning chef Adam Handling MBE describes his Cornish pub (named in reference to his Scottish heritage) as *'a den to escape to in the countryside'*.

The Tartan Fox, on a 30-acre site in rural Cornwall, joins the chef's growing family of determinedly sustainable dining venues. It's surrounded by an idyllic kitchen garden bursting with herbs, wildflowers, veg, fruit and beans – all used to create memorable meals while reducing supply-chain emissions.

Fellow GBM alumni and flame-cooking maestro Andi Tuck heads up the kitchen.

Start a visit with snacks of sourdough bread with chicken butter or a haggis scotch egg. Mains capture the locale and chef's culinary style in dishes such as lightly steamed Newlyn cod, served with tomatoes and Cornish cockles.

Further Scottish connections are found on the pudding line-up: try the zhuzhed-up version of a deep-fried Mars bar with the added indulgences of salted caramel and honeycomb.

Visiting on a Sunday? Luxury roasts include lemon and thyme half roast chicken, hot-smoked moorland beef and roast pork belly with apricot and sage – complete with all the trimmings. Next-day pies and specials are made using repurposed leftover ingredients to reduce waste and keep the menu ever-changing.

Trencherman's tip

A luxury tipi with fire chimneys is used for foodie gatherings, feasts and private hire, while a renovated barn hosts private dining, weddings and events. The busy roster includes fireside feasts, cooking masterclasses, seasonal markets, dried flower workshops, yoga mornings and art workshops with local creatives.

Chef **Adam Handling MBE** | 3-course dinner from **£43** | Seats **65**
tartanfoxpub.co.uk | Carvynick Farm, A3058, Newquay, Cornwall, TR8 5AF | **01637 800023**

17 Fistral Beach Hotel and Spa

Grown-ups-only glamour

This chic hotel's two-AA-rosette restaurant, contemporary spa and sublime sea views make it a popular find for discerning foodies looking for a fabulous place to stay.

The ocean-facing Dune Restaurant deserves top spot on any Newquay holiday itinerary. Guests can drink in panoramic views of the big blue while experiencing new head chef Pablo Borruto's cooking, which is packed with local produce.

Explore culinary creations with a Cornish twist, such as scallop with crispy pork belly, carrot and anise, soy glaze and sesame; lamb with salsify, artichoke purée, wild mushrooms and madeira sauce; and the earl grey ice-cream sandwich with pears, raisins and Sauternes syrup.

The surfy hotel has a luxury-resort vibe thanks to its incredible views, contemporary styling and rock-star extras, so there's no compromise

for those swapping the south of France for the Cornish coast. Overlooking Newquay's sweeping Fistral Beach, the bar and restaurant's panoramic windows offer guests rolling coverage of surfers riding the waves.

After a relaxing day of pampering in the Fistral Spa, kick off the evening with drinks in the Bay Bar. The experienced team serve signature cocktails such as Rose Garden (a concoction of St-Germain elderflower liqueur, Hendrick's Gin, lime juice and homemade rose syrup) as well as local craft beers.

Trencherman's tip

The vegan menu goes above and beyond to provide plant-based diners with creative options like salt-baked heritage beetroot tartlet with dukkah and herb salad.

Chef **Pablo Borruto** | 3-course dinner from **£50** | Seats 50 | Bedrooms 71 | Room rate from **£175** | **EV charging**
fistralbeachhotel.co.uk | Esplanade Road, Newquay, Cornwall, TR7 1PT | **01637 852221**

18 Ugly Butterfly 2.0 by Adam Handling

New chapter for no-waste restaurant

Ugly Butterfly made waves at its former home at Carbis Bay and is now sparking surprise and delight at a new residence.

At the iconic five-star Headland Hotel, which overlooks Fistral Beach, former *Great British Menu* champion Adam Handling MBE (and his OG team) deliver a very special experience. Guests can expect impeccable food from boundary-pushing chefs, wines recommended by experienced sommeliers and service from an uber-efficient front-of-house team.

Adam has a bold vision for sustainable British luxury and evolves the concept here with a 4x4 menu. Four starters, four middles, four mains and four desserts allow guests to create their own journey through the South West larder. Theatrical touches abound, with a Champagne trolley to kick things off, an infusions trolley to close, and plenty of magic in between.

Culinary highlights include bluefin tuna with preserved truffles and elderflower, Adam's signature lobster and wagyu dish which utilises sweet, small St Ives lobsters, and freshly baked Cornish apple tart – served tableside.

No visit is complete without sampling the legendary snacks, crafted from offcuts and trimmings into tiny bites of beauty.

Trencherman's tip

Ugly Butterfly's nearest sibling is The Tartan Fox near Newquay, but those heading further afield should schedule a visit to Adam's other enterprises. Michelin-starred Frog restaurant, Eve bar and Adam Handling Chocolate Shop are all to be found at London's Covent Garden, while The Loch & The Tyne pub is in Old Windsor.

Chef **Adam Handling MBE** | 3-course dinner from **£100** | Seats **42 inside, 24 outside, 26 bar** Bedrooms **86** | Room rate from **£195** | **EV charging**

uglybutterfly.co.uk | The Headland, Fistral Beach, Newquay, Cornwall, TR7 1EW | **01637 839739**

19 Scarlet Hotel

Coastal eco sanctuary

Scarlet Hotel has long been a pioneer of sustainability in the South West. The luxury eco hotel balances ethical sustainability with utter indulgence, so it's no surprise it was voted Best Hotel at the Trencherman's Awards 2024.

The hotel and restaurant provide a sophisticated yet green-leaning experience where guests can luxuriate in low-impact feasting and lazing.

Healthy hedonism rules in the kitchen where head chef Jack Clayton's passion for seafood and sustainability marries perfectly with the environmental ethos of the hotel.

His philosophy centres on the journey of individual Cornish ingredients, which are largely seasonal, foraged (the chefs scour the coastline and hotel grounds daily) or sourced from small suppliers. These are showcased in dishes such as netted Cornish turbot stuffed with a sea lettuce and nasturtium mousse, served with broccoli and anchovy puree, crispy hasselback Cornish early potatoes, verjus-compressed grapes, coastal herbs and nasturtium oil.

A carefully curated drinks list includes wines from producers with organic and biodynamic viticulture at their heart, along with finds from indie breweries and distilleries that share Scarlet's low-impact approach.

Trencherman's tip

Bliss out with a bespoke treatment at the eco-luxe clifftop spa.

Chef **Jack Clayton** | 3-course dinner from **£75** | Seats **56** | Bedrooms **37** | Room rate from **£250** | **EV charging**
scarlethotel.co.uk | Tredragon Road, Mawgan Porth, Cornwall, TR8 4DQ | **01637 861800**

20 Barnaby's

Vine dining

Down a country lane, past grapevines, apple trees and roaming Southdown sheep, this home of hyper-local seasonal sharing plates is ensconced within family-run Trevibban Mill vineyard and orchards.

Sister site to the hugely popular Prawn on the Lawn (POTL), Barnaby's specialises in flavour-packed sharing dishes that are every bit as memorable as the location.

Taking his lead from POTL owner and exec chef Rick Toogood, head chef Eddie Thomson sources almost all his produce from nearby farms and fishermen, and neighbouring veg and salad growers. They also harvest a lot of veggies from Rick's polytunnel in St Kew.

Chances are the ingredients in dishes like crab toast with muhammara, watercress and walnuts; mushrooms with whipped tahini and

spiced gremolata; and Trevibban cull yaw kofta with smoked chilli oil and garlic yogurt will have arrived at Barnaby's not much earlier than its eager diners.

The team also butcher and make their own charcuterie in-house, serve beers from the microbrewery next door, and offer a sparkling pink Pinot Noir wine grown on vines that surround the restaurant.

Trencherman's tip

Make time for pre- and post-meal drinks in the festoon-lit wildflower garden. The cocktail menu is as seasonal as the food, and the Frozen Margarita is a must-try.

Left to right: Katie Toogood, Eddie Thomson and Jade Dunphy of Barnaby's, Mike Ellis of Alliance

Chef **Eddie Thomson** | 3-course dinner from **£45** | Seats **50**

prawnonthelawn.com/restaurant/barnabys | Trevibban Mill, Dark Lane, Near Padstow, PL27 7SE | 07926 128148

21 Paul Ainsworth at No6

Star-quality dining

As the jewel in the crown of chef-restaurateur Paul Ainsworth's small Cornish empire, No6 is a Michelin-starred dining experience that showcases modern British cooking at its best.

Ainsworth learnt his craft working with legends Gary Rhodes, Gordon Ramsay and Marcus Wareing, before honing his signature style at this Georgian townhouse.

Intimate, romantic and delivering impeccable standards of service, No6 sets a gastronomic benchmark in the South West.

Start with an aperitif and a pintxo or two at the upstairs bar (named after Paul's daughter CiCi) before taking a seat in the main restaurant with its views of the kitchen, or at a table in the Florence Parker private dining room. In both locations, the food takes centre stage, served via a duo of experiences. Opt for the wider culinary journey through the kitchen with the seven-course tasting menu or capture the essence of No6 in a more flexible format with the à la carte menu.

Using only the finest local produce, the showstopping dishes taste as good as they look. Land & River is a prime example. This dish of smoked eel and Golden Oscietra caviar reflects the full array of flavours and techniques that define the No6 approach.

A reimagined tournedos rossini, first created by Paul in 2018, uses Creedy Carver chicken finished with sauce brioche, while the indulgent Pie 'n' Chips for two is layered with Cornish Moor beef and Porthilly oyster.

Trencherman's tip

For the full Ainsworth experience, stay at Paul's 18th-century Padstow Townhouse.

Left to right: Marc Megilley of Trevethan, Paul Ainsworth, Carly Fordy of Trevethan

Chef **Paul Ainsworth** | 3-course dinner from **£105** | Seats 38 | Bedrooms 6 | Room rate from **£375**
paul-ainsworth.co.uk/number6 | 6 Middle Street, Padstow, Cornwall, PL28 8AP | **01841 532093**

22 The Seafood Restaurant

50 years of the longstanding classic

'Little did Rick and I ever imagine, when we opened our doors in 1975, we would still be here 50 years later,' **Jill Stein says as The Seafood Restaurant marks its half-century on the South West dining scene.**

But with its winning mix of smart–casual dishes, ultra-fresh local seafood and global wines, it's no surprise that the Stein family's flagship restaurant has become such a longstanding classic.

A fiercely entrepreneurial spirit and a lack of ego may be partly to thank for the restaurant's ongoing success. Those values have been at the forefront since day one, as Rick and Jill grew the business organically in Padstow and beyond. Today, they continue to be upheld by their sons Charlie, Jack and Ed.

Join the discerning pilgrims who journey to Padstow to sample dishes such as classic lobster thermidor, cooked in a light cream and Noilly Prat sauce with fines herbes and parmesan, and served with thin-cut chips. Dishes change seasonally, depending on what produce is delivered to head chef Pete Murt's kitchen door, so there's always something new to sample.

Dining at a table in the restaurant is delightful, but those swinging by for a quick bite and a glass of wine should perch at the central zinc bar and watch the restaurant action unfold.

Trencherman's tip

Guests can celebrate the restaurant's milestone by booking the Taste of 50 Years menu, getting away from it all with a Golden Celebration break in one of the coastally inspired rooms, or trying their hand at something from the anniversary cookbook.

Chef **Pete Murt** | 3-course dinner from **£55** | Seats **130** | Bedrooms **16** | Room rate from **£185**
rickstein.com | Riverside, Padstow, Cornwall, PL28 8BY | **01841 532700**

23 2 Fore Street Restaurant

Foodie magnet in Mousehole

In-the-know gourmets make a beeline for this chic bistro right on the fishing village's harbour.

Sit inside and drink in the stunning views across Mount's Bay or, if it's sunny, head to the secluded courtyard garden. The alfresco area has its own microclimate and is perfect for basking in the sun with a glass of chilled fizz and a dish from a menu of classics. If the oceanside setting stirs a hunger for seafood, the signature twice-baked Newlyn crab and parmesan soufflé or hot Cornish seafood plate with crab mayonnaise is sure to delight.

Only the freshest Cornish fish and locally sourced meat and veggies make their way onto the menus of Raymond Blanc-trained chef patron Joe Wardell.

While this slipway-side dining spot is a real catch for dinner, those heading to the beach opposite are welcome to swing by for morning coffee or lunch. The midday menu includes breezier sustenance such as lemon-sole burgers, cheese and chutney toasties, and crab sarnies.

Anyone considering a weekender in Mousehole should check out The Boatwatch, the restaurant's cosy apartment on the harbour. Maritime decor, a wood-burning stove and open-plan living area makes it a special find in the town.

Trencherman's tip

Grab goodies to-go from the sister deli shop, which stocks Da Bara Bakery treats, Freehand coffee, Moomaid of Zennor Ice Cream and wine from Enotria&Coe.

Chef **Joe Wardell** | 3-course dinner from **£42** | Seats **34**
2forestreet.co.uk | 2 Fore Street, Mousehole, Penzance, Cornwall, TR19 6QU | **01736 731164**

24 St Michaels Resort

Nourishing body and soul

Leafy subtropical gardens, two restaurants and a lush spa make this smart resort in Falmouth a must-visit for those looking to feed both body and soul.

Experience the culinary delights from talented head chef Dave Waters (pictured opposite) in the roomy Brasserie on the Bay, with its coastal views of Falmouth Bay and the resort's stunning gardens.

Dave was born and bred in Cornwall. As a child, he fished off Mousehole with his grandad, and as a young chef spent six years with Nathan Outlaw, sharpening his seafood skills to a razor-clam edge. It's fair to say the county's ocean bounty runs through his veins.

He approaches his craft with both technical precision and respect for the produce sourced from Cornwall's verdant fields and generous waters. In this setting, Dave showcases both in menus that centre on sparklingly fresh seafood.

Experience a taste of the coast by starting dinner with three hand-dived, half-shell Cornish scallops served with pumpkin seeds, coriander, chilli, parmesan and spring onion. Follow with whichever fat and juicy fish has been landed nearby that morning.

For alternative all-day dining, head next door to Nourish. Here, wholesome and deliciously down-to-earth food, from pizza to healthy small plates, is complemented by good coffee and smoothies.

Trencherman's tip

Further entertainment can be found by wandering through the gardens, lazing in the largest hydrothermal pool in the South West, getting a rejuvenating treatment in the spa and working up a sweat at the high-calibre Health Club. Outdoor thrills include sea swimming and paddleboarding in the bay.

Left to right: Pete Churchill and Tim Fryer (both formerly of St Michaels Resort), Tom Eaton of Classic Fine Foods

Chef **Dave Waters** | 3-course dinner from **£60** | Seats **80** | Bedrooms **96** | Room rate from **£200** | **EV charging**
stmichaelsresort.com | Gyllyngvase Beach, Falmouth, Cornwall, TR11 4NB | **01326 312707**

25 Falmouth Arms

French classics in the countryside

Kevin Viner made history in 1993 by earning Cornwall's first Michelin star at Pennypots in Blackwater – an honour he retained for seven consecutive years.

Following this, he spent years consulting and cooking for high-profile clients including the Royal Family and the Prince and Princess of Monaco. He then returned to Cornwall and has now revived the Pennypots name within The Falmouth Arms in Ladock, the rural inn he runs with his wife Jill.

The couple have revitalised the historic 17th-century coaching inn, retaining its beamed ceilings and wonky walls while adding their own distinctive style.

Kevin's menus, refined over decades, showcase a select number of elegantly crafted classics made from Cornwall's very best produce. Cooked by Kevin and served by Jill, highlights include the twice-baked West Country cheese soufflé, roasted lobster with orange fennel and basil risotto, and pavlova with lemon posset and Cornish mead-marinated raspberries.

Dinner is served Wednesday to Saturday, while on Sundays the inn takes on its true pub persona by serving up generous traditional roasts.

Not ready to leave? Settle in for the night in one of four character-packed ensuite guest rooms. In the morning, enjoy a breakfast feast ranging from continental favourites to hearty cooked dishes.

Trencherman's tip

Take note of the chef's expert recommendations for the perfect food and wine pairings.

Chef **Kevin Viner** | 3-course dinner from **£35** | Seats **40** | Bedrooms **3** | Room rate from **£95**
falmoutharms.co.uk | Coaching Inn, Ladock, Truro, Cornwall, TR2 4PG | **01726 882319**

26 Halwyn

New concept in Cornish hospitality

This game-changing new opening on the north Cornwall coast puts a bold spin on casual dining in a wild, rural location.

Founder Will Eustice has created a strikingly good destination for gathering and feasting, housed on his family's farmland near Newquay.

The eating takes place in a large open-plan restaurant built around exposed oak beams, a cosy log burner and sweeping countryside views. It's here that chef Matt Haggath (ex-Idle Rocks and Savoy Grill) serves a casual menu rooted in fire, flame (the Josper charcoal grill is the workhorse of the kitchen) and provenance.

Top-notch ingredients include beef from the Trevowah herd, reared a few fields away by Will's cousin. Warm up for supper with winning snacks such as potted beef brisket with beef-fat toast, horseradish and tarragon, or smoked lamb-shoulder fritters with romesco, pine nut, basil and whipped ricotta.

Meaty mains – think big cut steaks; barbecue spatchcock chicken with radish and shallot salad, chimichurri and fries; and pork chops with garlic and sage marinade plus seasonal greens and barbecue mustard ketchup – take star turns on the menu. Fish dishes, such as pan-seared skate fillet with lardons, crispy kale, onion and mushroom velouté and chive oil, are equally fresh and carefully sourced.

Halwyn is a space for gathering. For many visitors the vehicle for connection is the whizzy golf offering (a separate entity from the restaurant) comprising a state-of-the-art Trackman driving range and a contemporary take on mini golf. No expertise is required as this is all about having fun – both on the range and in the restaurant.

Trencherman's tip

Gather with like-minded gourmets at Halwyn's feast nights, which run throughout the year.

Chef **Matthew Haggath** | 3-course dinner from **£40** | Seats **60**
halwyn.co.uk | Halwyn Road, Crantock, Cornwall, TR8 5TR | **01637 520201**

27 The Headland Hotel & Spa

Iconic coastal hotel with cool creds

With a history dating back to 1900 and a jaw-dropping vantage point on cliffs above Newquay's Fistral Beach, this Grade II-listed coastal icon may look heritage in style, but enjoys state-of-the-art amenities.

Beneath the traditional facade and timeless charm, guests of the five-star luxury resort will discover impeccably appointed rooms, a spa, an AquaClub swimming and wellbeing complex, and three restaurants catering to every taste.

The hotel's flagship restaurant, RenMor, is overseen by respected executive chef Gavin Edney. It's a light, contemporary space with floor-to-ceiling windows that make the most of the Atlantic views and stunning sunsets.

The feast for the eyes extends to sumptuous dishes such as Mora Farm tomatoes with Newquay harbour crab, Cornish kelp and chilled tomato dashi, and line-caught wild sea bass bourguignon with smoked celeriac, Cornish chanterelles and black plum sauce. Desserts like the peach melba ice-cream sundae provide a decadent finale.

RenMor is also open for breakfast, lunch and afternoon tea. The hotel's other must-visit restaurant is new arrival The Ugly Butterfly by Adam Handling (in what was previously The Terrace Restaurant), which deals in hyper-seasonal menus and uber-creative cooking.

Trencherman's tip

Stay in one of The Headland's beautiful Sea View Cottages. They offer full access to the hotel facilities and spa but with tucked-away privacy.

Chef **Gavin Edney** | 3-course dinner from **£55** | Seats **150** | Bedrooms **86** | Room rate from **£200** | **EV charging**
headlandhotel.co.uk | Fistral Beach, Headland Road, Newquay, TR7 1EW | **01637 872211**

28 Bedruthan Hotel & Spa

Colourful cliffside retreat

The sister establishment and neighbour to grown-ups-only Scarlet Hotel shares the same sustainable ethos as its sibling. Here, however, it's packaged as a Scandi-inspired retreat for families and creatives.

A swish spa, art classes, yoga sessions, wellbeing gatherings and feasting events make the hotel pulse with connectivity and innovation. There's also plenty to keep kids entertained, while everyone will enjoy the quality cooking.

Eating options come in a variety of forms. At laid-back and brightly coloured Wild Cafe, locally caught mussels cooked in a white wine sauce are a perennial hit.

There's also a minimal-waste bakery, where favourites include cinnamon buns, rosemary and sea-salt twists and sourdough loaves – a selection of which are made without bleached or refined flours and sugars.

Restaurant Ogo ('cave' in Cornish) charms with its daily changing menu, which leverages the freshest local and seasonal produce. This is where the team of chefs create a veritable feast of sea, garden and field. An amazing 90–95 per cent of the dishes are made using Cornish produce and influenced by foraged finds on the coastline.

The creative and Cornish-led menu is matched in provenance creds by an exclusively Cornish wine list of organic and biodynamic finds.

Trencherman's tip

The golden sands of Mawgan Porth beach are a mere stone's throw away and Bedruthan is also near the South West Coast Path – perfect, as the hotel is also dog friendly.

Chef **Georgia Mugford** | 3-course dinner from **£50** | Seats **76 (Ogo), 170 (Wild Cafe)** | Bedrooms **110**
Room rate from **£90** | **EV charging**
bedruthan.com | Mawgan Porth, Cornwall, TR8 4BU | **01637 861200**

29 Prawn on the Lawn

Phenomenally fresh seafood small plates

A sprawling menu of small plates that everyone will want to dig into – think hake with truffle oil, parmesan, cauliflower and porcini crumb; lemon sole with 'nduja and tarragon; and crispy chilli monkfish with sesame, ginger and garlic – has made this one of Cornwall's most notable seafood restaurants.

For a decade, this POTL Padstow site (the original is in Islington) has brought piscatorial thrills to Duke Street. Its refined menus are updated daily and dictated by what the Cornish fishermen land each morning, so no two visits are ever quite the same.

Working closely with chef Izzy Joscelyne, founder and chef Rick Toogood favours sustainable fish and shellfish species. The pair supplement the day's catch with hyper-fresh veg from the restaurant's own raised beds and produce grown by Ross Geach of Padstow Kitchen Garden.

All of the delicious morsels at this bijou seafood bar are complemented by local wines from nearby Trevibban Mill and beers from Padstow Brewing Co. and Bluntrock.

Trencherman's tip

POTL fans will want to schedule a trip to the two sister sites. Seafood bar Little Prawn is just across the street (menu must-tries include scallops, octopus, fresh lobster and Cornish som tam), while Barnaby's restaurant is housed at nearby Trevibban Mill vineyard.

Chef **Izzy Joscelyne** | 3-course dinner from **£50** | Seats **25**
prawnonthelawn.com | 11 Duke Street, Padstow, Cornwall, PL28 8AB | 07926 128148

30 St Tudy Inn

Next-gen Cornish cooking

This iconic dining pub has long held a special place in the hearts of those in the know, having built a formidable reputation in the 2010s under Emily Scott. A decade on, the St Tudy Inn is enjoying another exciting new era, this time under head chef George Buckley and his band of bright young Cornish chefs.

Kitchens have been George's sanctuary from the age of seven, as he grew up helping his dad at the family restaurant. As a teenager, he worked at The Mill House before claiming his first head-chef position at a local golf club. His big break came at Tintagel Brewery Bar & Bistro, which won a coveted finalist spot for Best Newcomer at the Trencherman's Awards 2023.

At St Tudy, George leads a dynamic kitchen crew who are clearly having a lot of fun with this venture, while also creating some seriously good food. The dishes that flow from the pass exude a confidence that belies George's informal training.

Starters might include Cornish white crab with brown crab emulsion, almond and cucumber, while mains such as hake with chanterelles, herb gnocchi, wild garlic and butter sauce showcase skill and seasonal ingredients. For plant-based diners, roasted maitake mushroom with green tahini and teriyaki is a flavour-forward find.

The pub's AA-rosette-awarded rooms in a converted barn offer a cosy retreat just steps from the action and turn dinner into a foodie getaway. Live music and a busy calendar of seasonal events are further reasons to visit.

Trencherman's tip

Look out for excellent value lunchtime offers, especially in the low and shoulder seasons.

Chef **George Buckley** | 3-course dinner from **£50** | Seats **80** | Bedrooms **4** | Room rate from **£100**
sttudyinn.com | St Tudy, Bodmin, Cornwall, PL30 3NN | **01208 850656**

31 The Sardine Factory

Sustainable seafood on the harbour

In the 19th century, Looe's Sardine Factory did exactly what it says on the tin: when fishermen shouted *'Hevva!'*, it meant shoals of pilchards (known locally as Cornish sardines) had been sighted, and the boats would bring in the catch for processing.

Chef-owner Ben Palmer had cherished a dream of opening a restaurant in his hometown, and in July 2018 he transformed this historic harbourside building into an 80-cover restaurant.

Ben's culinary skills have bagged him a number of notable awards, including Best Chef in the Trencherman's Awards 2024 and a Michelin Bib Gourmand. Ben also made it all the way to the banquet in the BBC's *Great British Menu* 2024, while further BBC coverage comes in the drama *Beyond Paradise*, in which the restaurant features as the Ten Mile Kitchen.

Ben specialises in creating sustainable fish dishes using produce from Looe's fish market (located opposite the restaurant).

Menu stalwarts include smoked haddock scotch egg, pimped with curried mayo, gem lettuce and citrus fennel, and Cornish crab linguine with chilli, garlic, basil, tomato, parmesan and pangritata. Looe lobster, grilled in garlic butter with lemon, is another Sardine Factory staple. If raw seafood floats your boat, pick the Cornish bluefin tuna ceviche, while dessert fans will swoon over the baked apple tarte tatin for two.

Take the scenic route to lunch – or the newly introduced Sunday brunch – along the Looe Valley branch line, one of the UK's most tranquil railway lines.

Trencherman's tip

Get your Greek on by booking a table at sister restaurant Yamas in East Looe.

Chef **Ben Palmer** | 3-course dinner from **£25** | Seats **80**

thesardinefactorylooe.com | The Quay, West Looe, Cornwall, PL13 2BX | **01503 770262**

32 Yamas

Greek and Cornish fusion

Greek dishes packed with Cornish ingredients make for a sublime collision of cultures at this East Looe restaurant. Its name is taken from the Greek toast *'to our health!'* and helps set the continental tone.

Set right on the water's edge, Yamas is heaven for gourmets who subscribe to the idea that good food tastes all the sweeter with a noseful of sea air and a backdrop of higgledy-piggledy fishermen's cottages. Add pared-back interiors of whites and neutrals, and the result is a perfect reflection of luminous Cornish skies and simple Greek style.

From expertly slow-cooked beef-cheek stifado to crispy calamari, creamy moussaka, and melt-in-the-mouth parcels comprising filo, feta and spinach, expect all the classics found in a true Greek taverna. Everything, down to the simplicity of the humble Greek salad, is carefully curated to maximise authenticity and flavour.

Yamas is the sister site of West Looe success story The Sardine Factory. It's co-owned by Nikos Oikonomopoulos (the chef at the helm) and Ben Palmer (of *Great British Menu* fame and winner of Best Chef at the Trencherman's Awards 2024). The pair's shared vision and Nikos' culinary kudos meant Yamas was always destined to be a quality dining destination.

Trencherman's tip

Pitch up early for your table and spend time perusing the deli shelves of Greek goodies or indulging in a Passionfruit Martini with a view at the upstairs bar and terrace.

Chef **Nikos Oikonomopoulos** | 3-course dinner from **£30** | Seats **40**
yamaslooe.com | The Quay, Looe, Cornwall, PL13 1AH | **01503 770262**

Devon

Devon

Numbers on the map correspond to the numbers next to the restaurants in the guide.

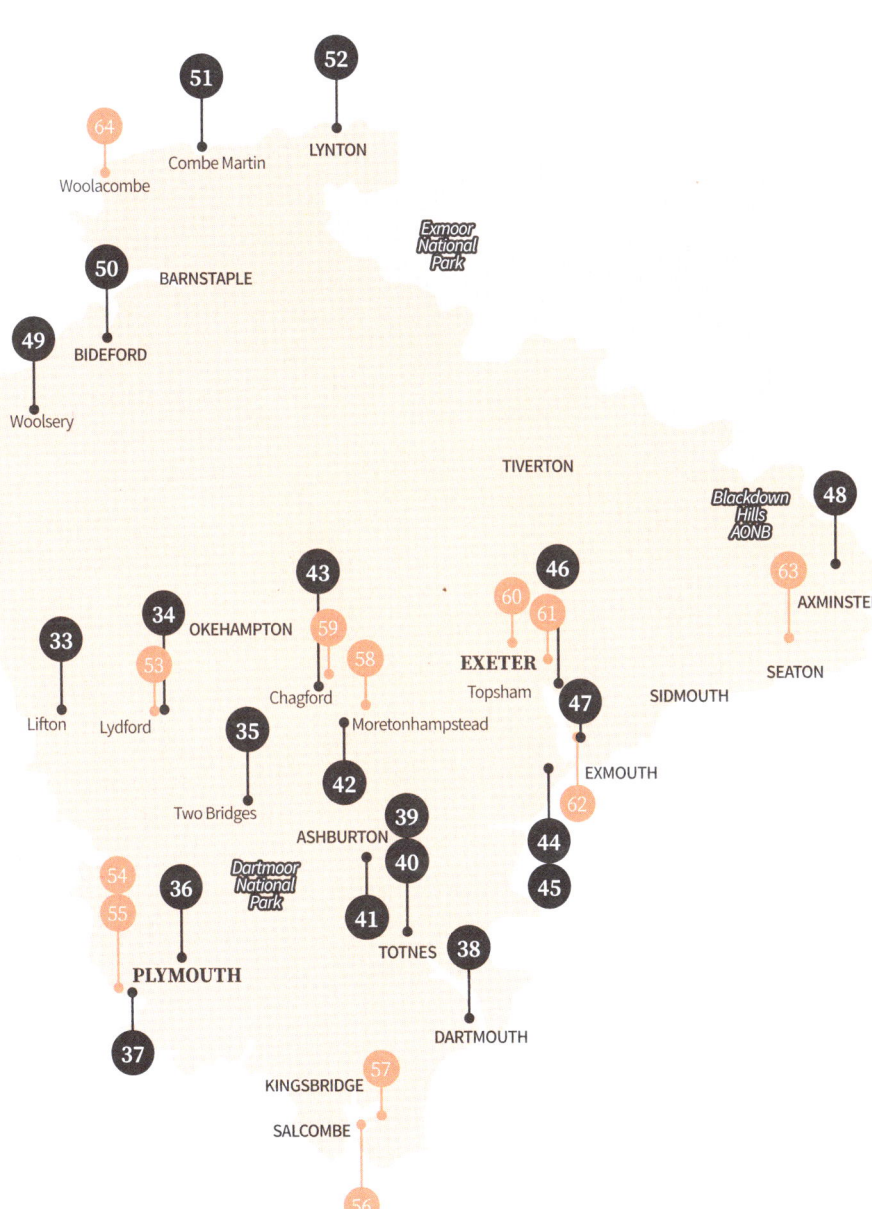

64 Woolacombe

51 Combe Martin

52 LYNTON

Exmoor National Park

50 BARNSTAPLE

49 BIDEFORD

Woolsery

TIVERTON

Blackdown Hills AONB

48

63 AXMINSTER

SEATON

43

46

34 OKEHAMPTON

33

59

60

61

EXETER

Topsham

47

SIDMOUTH

Lifton

53

Lydford

58

Chagford

Moretonhampstead

35

EXMOUTH

62

Two Bridges

42

ASHBURTON

44

54

36

Dartmoor National Park

39

45

55

40

PLYMOUTH

41

TOTNES

38

37

KINGSBRIDGE

57

DARTMOUTH

SALCOMBE

56

Locations are approximate

Devon **73**

33 The Arundell Arms

Country pursuits meet culinary prowess

Straddling the Devon-Cornwall border in the sleepy village of Lifton, The Arundell Arms is a traditional country inn which, for generations, has provided hospitality in the countryside.

More than just a pub and restaurant with rooms, The Arundell Arms also claims 22 miles of privately managed riverbank, a lake and one of the best fly-fishing schools in the country. Anglers return year after year to wade into its waters and enjoy the therapy that comes from a day on the river.

However, arriving laden with rods and reels is not a prerequisite for a visit. Those more drawn to land-based pursuits will find themselves surrounded by scenery that's crying out for exploration.

At the end of a day's country pursuits, roaring fires, flagstone floors and a cosy library (or the English country garden in summer) await those congregating for pre-dinner drinks.

Dinner in the chandeliered dining room is delightful thanks to the trad decor and chef Phillip Old's seasonal menus featuring local and wild ingredients. Dishes include gin-smoked trout with watermelon, feta and zesty lime salad, and pan-fried line-caught local fish of the day with fennel and a garlic and lemon sauce vierge.

While freshly caught trout often appears, there's no farmed salmon on the menu – the establishment was one of the first supporters of the Off The Table campaign.

Trencherman's tip

The good food, clutch of quintessentially English guest rooms and fleet of Tesla chargers make The Arundell Arms an oasis for travellers journeying through the South West.

Chef **Phillip Old** | 3-course dinner from **£45** | Seats **60** | Bedrooms **21** | Room rate from **£175**
thearundell.com | Fore Street, Lifton, Devon, PL16 0AA | **01566 784666**

34 The Dartmoor Inn at Lydford

Sophisticated pub dining

There are countless country inns where you can rock up at the bar in your wellies following a moorland yomp. But for those seeking something smarter than post-hike pub grub, The Dartmoor Inn strikes the balance between cosy bar and smart restaurant and has made a name for itself among savvy foodies looking for contemporary Dartmoor dining.

Since taking over the pub in 2019, chef Jay Barker-Jones and wife Tess (front of house) have bagged a *Michelin Guide* listing and racked up various awards, including Best Pub at both the Trencherman's Awards 2024 and the Food Drink Devon Awards 2023.

In the kitchen, Jay focuses on crafting refined fare, which is served in a thoroughly unstuffy setting. His ever-developing menus reflect what's in season and produced locally. For a

taste of Dartmoor, opt for starters like tender wood pigeon accompanied by Jerusalem artichoke, mushrooms and blackberries, followed by superstar mains like locally shot red venison loin with haunch ragout, salt-baked celeriac, red cabbage, pickled walnut, charred Tenderstem and red wine.

The culinary offering also includes a cracking seafood selection: dishes such as sea bass with sauté potatoes, garlic tiger prawns, samphire, peppers, chorizo and romesco are manna for fish fans.

Trencherman's tip

The drinks experience is as carefully crafted as the food. The expansive wine list is curated by nearby Tavistock's Sovereign Wines and includes a global array of wineries. There's also an excellent selection of cocktails and non-alcoholic options.

Chef **Jay Barker-Jones** | 3-course dinner from **£39** | Seats **60** | Bedrooms **3** | Room rate from **£119**
dartmoorinn.com | Moorside, Lydford, Okehampton, Devon, EX20 4AY | **01822 820221**

35 Two Bridges Hotel

Destination Dartmoor dining

Looking for a luxurious base from which to explore the moor, or seeking a cosy bolthole with roaring fires and superb dining? This hotel and two-AA-rosette restaurant amid the wilds of Dartmoor offers a guaranteed great escape.

The classic interiors at Two Bridges Hotel are perfect in this moorland environment. Ornate fireplaces, grand old clocks and paintings, polished brass and copper, and a well-stocked bar are precisely what you'd hope to discover after a day tramping over the tussocky hills. Even in bleak midwinter, the attractive hotel is an oasis of hospitality.

Within this characterful setting, talented head chef Josh Chan crafts dishes packed with the very best local ingredients. The team try to use as many hyper-local suppliers as possible to curate moor-centric menus featuring the likes of Dartmoor Farmers dry-aged beef fillet with bacon jam, savoy cabbage heart, bone marrow and smoked jus, and Creedy Carver duck breast with confit duck leg, braised chicory and duck jus.

The hearty favourites on the lunch menu are just the thing after a bracing stomp, while in the evening guests can upgrade to the four-course signature menu for an elevated experience.

Fine wines complement the cooking, and the hotel often hosts wine-pairing dinners. The Two Bridges Devon cream tea is equally noteworthy and best devoured in the garden.

Trencherman's tip

Stay over in one of the comfortable bedrooms, which come with four-poster beds and antique furniture.

Chef **Josh Chan** | 3-course dinner from **£40** | Seats **60** | Bedrooms **32** | Room rate from **£135** | **EV charging**
twobridges.co.uk | Dartmoor National Park, Devon, PL20 6SW | **01822 892300**

36 Àclèaf

Novel Michelin-starred meals

Grade II-listed Boringdon Hall Hotel in Devon is steeped in history thanks to its Elizabethan architecture and inclusion in the *Domesday Book*. However, it's also home to an ultra-contemporary food offering in the form of its Michelin-starred, four-AA-rosette restaurant Àclèaf.

Anyone who has had the pleasure of eating chef Scott Paton's food will be familiar with his eye for artful plating and talent for palate-pleasing combinations. He homes in on hyper-seasonal produce to create dishes that are both imaginative and rooted in tradition.

Scott says: *'Dining at Àclèaf is interactive – a menu with twists and turns along the way.'* The focus is fully on ingredients and the chef expends serious energy sourcing the best produce for his novel dining experiences.

Hero ingredients on the four-course and seven-course menus include the likes of Highland Wagyu paired with peas and pancetta, scallop given zing by ginger and kaffir lime, and mango with coconut and yuzu.

Scott's nose for exceptional drink pairings is showcased in an English-led wine flight that takes the dining experience next-level.

Trencherman's tip

Book one of the boutique bedrooms or suites to make a grand gourmet getaway of your visit, and spend time soaking in the award-winning, state-of-the-art (and adults-only) Gaia Spa before dinner.

Chef **Scott Paton** | 4-course dinner from **£120** | Seats **40** | Bedrooms **55** | Room rate from **£200** | **EV charging**
acleaf.co.uk | Boringdon Hall Hotel, Boringdon Hill, Plymouth, Devon, PL7 4DP | **01752 344455**

37 Barbican Kitchen

Modern dining in a historical location

Brothers Chris and James Tanner have long been mainstays on the Plymouth dining scene, and in 2026 they celebrate 20 years at Barbican Kitchen.

Situated inside an ancient building that's also home to the Plymouth Gin Distillery (and supposedly where the Pilgrim Fathers spent their last night before setting sail on the *Mayflower*), the restaurant's location makes for an inspiring experience even before sampling the food. The original stone walls of the venue are complemented by contemporary styling; the result is a successful marriage of old and new.

A relaxed vibe sets expectations for a smart-casual menu and the team deliver in style. Dishes are built around locally sourced ingredients such as fish landed by Looe dayboats and meat from Philip Warren Butchers in Launceston. This fine fare is crafted into creations such as tuna tartare with compressed watermelon, miso mayonnaise, ponzu, puffed rice and nori.

Committed carnivores will revel in the likes of slow-cooked beef short rib with a bone marrow and horseradish crust, smoked cream potato, glazed onion, pork puffs and red wine sauce.

Plant-based visitors will be pleased by the superb selection of veg-centric dishes, all crafted using hyper-fresh ingredients from the surrounding Devon countryside.

Trencherman's tip

Booking for lunch? Barbican Kitchen is open at lunchtime on Friday and Saturday. Dinner service runs from Tuesday to Saturday.

Chef **Martyn Compton** | 3-course dinner from **£26** | Seats **100**
barbicankitchen.com | Plymouth Gin Distillery, 60 Southside Street, Plymouth, Devon, PL1 2LQ | **01752 604448**

38 Andria

Small plates with European flair

Named after the Puglian town of chef-owner Luca Berardino's ancestors, Andria is where the talented chef turns his memories and food experiences into unconventional tasting menus and a daily line-up of carefully crafted small plates.

The restaurant has garnered much attention since opening in 2020, testament to Luca and team's determination to push boundaries and offer a distinctive dining experience.

Sample the likes of burnt courgette with whipped tahini, caramelised garlic, chilli and mint followed by local goat's curd (made to order for the restaurant) with beetroot marmalade, oats and blossom honey.

Above the restaurant, a chef's table experience offers diners something a little different. Here, eight guests spend the evening in Luca's company being wined, dined and entertained while feasting on a tasting menu cooked and served from an open kitchen. The immersive supper is all about connection, so book a seat (not a table) to enjoy a menu flush with foraged finds from the coast and countryside in the company of other discerning diners.

For a more casual visit, the lunchtime set menu is excellent value, and the Sunday roast with all the trimmings is ultra popular.

Trencherman's tip

The fabulous food is complemented by a lively playlist, relaxed atmosphere and great wines – including a good selection by the glass.

Chef **Luca Berardino** | 3 course dinner from **£40** | Seats **32**

andriadartmouth.com | 5 Lower Street, Dartmouth, Devon, TQ6 9AJ | **01803 833222**

39 Circa

Ever-evolving culinary adventures

Inside the four walls of a historical Grade II-listed building in Totnes, light work is made of contemporary cooking using unusual ingredients.

Chef-director Rob Weeks has a firm grasp on seasonal food and flavours, favouring organic ingredients wherever possible.

Midweek dishes are all about small plates, with an emphasis on sharing cuts and ferments. The kitchen crew also favour cooking over open flame, which takes grilled foods next-level – especially Sundays' sharing-cut roasts.

The team are constantly looking to improve their zero-waste systems and are working towards being entirely self-sufficient. A market garden is flourishing, while ongoing developments include a mushroom grow-room and a dry store to expand the busy pickling and fermenting operation.

The aim? To guarantee wholesome and full-flavoured produce for standout dishes. Try such innovations as the lion's mane kebab of homemade sourdough flatbread, pan-roasted Dartington lion's mane mushrooms, hay butter, cider, spent-coffee glaze and shiitake mushroom served three ways (a decadent foam, preserved and raw).

More veggie wonders include fermented kalibos cabbage cooked in celeriac-skin oil and served with homemade gorse-flower crème fraîche, salt-baked and raw kohlrabi, a spruce emulsion, shiso leaf from The Husbandry School and fig-leaf oil.

Trencherman's tip

Got a friend who's a 'shroom fan? Champignon concoctions can be found across the menu, including in desserts such as lion's mane fudge.

Chef **Rob Weeks** | 3-course dinner from **£40** | Seats **40**

circadevon.co.uk | 26 High Street, Totnes, Devon, TQ9 5RY | **01803 868674**

40 Gather

Exciting field-to-fork dining

Any chef worth their salt knows where their produce comes from, yet the zealous team at this Totnes restaurant go the extra mile by foraging many of the ingredients on their menu. Their produce-led practices have seen Gather feature on Channel 4's *Remarkable Places to Eat* and receive two AA rosettes.

For chefs Harrison Brockington and Oli Rosier, showcasing the unique flavours of Devon's fields, shoreline, rivers and hedgerows is the underlying principle of everything they do. This deep connection with their environment is expressed in full and half tasting menus, tweaked daily and revised monthly to reflect what's in season.

Along with foraged finds, the pair choose local suppliers whose ethos aligns with the restaurant's climate-conscious principles. Meat reared in the South Hams comes courtesy of Christopher McCabe Butchers, while seasonal

and organic veg is supplied by a smallholding a few miles away.

Constant refinement and unshackled creativity result in dishes that appeal to the culinarily curious. Milk and honey parfait, for example, is crafted using locally sourced Buckfast Abbey honey and topped with wild flowers under an architectural tuile dome, while tender braised rabbit shoulder is encased within hand-shaped farfalle and elevated with wild garlic.

Both tasting options have an accompanying wine flight, but the team are always happy to suggest alternative pairings.

Trencherman's tip

Harrison won a whopping trio of awards at South West Chef of the Year 2024: Overall Chef of the Year, Professional Chef of the Year and Best Dish.

Chef **Harrison Brockington** | 3-course dinner from **£30** | Seats **25**
gathertotnes.com | 50 Fore Street, Totnes, Devon, TQ9 5RP | **01803 866666**

41 Le Vin Perdu

Fresh French vibes in Ashburton

This rotisserie-led restaurant in Ashburton takes its inspiration from the small neighbourhood bistros of France that change their menus weekly to reflect whatever's good, local, and in season.

Sibling to the Italian-style Emilia nearby, Le Vin Perdu hops the border into France for its flavour cues. However, it keeps the same laidback, neighbourhood vibe that's become the signature of Clare Lattin and Tom Hill's restaurants.

The rotisserie is the heart of the kitchen. Expect meltingly soft lamb shoulder in rosemary and anchovy butter, served with garlic-roasted parmentier potatoes, or sample luscious rotisserie chicken with garlic and herb butter, served with potatoes roasted in chicken fat.

Occupying one of Ashburton's ancient townhouses, Le Vin Perdu's light-filled dining room features a bar for aperitifs, plus larger tables for group and family dining. In the summer, feast outside in the garden. For an easygoing family feast, swing by for the rotisserie chicken Sunday lunch.

Where Le Vin Perdu brings French vibes, Emilia invites guests into an intimate open kitchen and dining space, serving a weekly changing menu of Italian plates (including a homemade pasta dish).

Both restaurants scour Dartmoor and the South Hams for hyper-local produce, which is treated with reverence by the creative kitchen team.

Trencherman's tip

Le Vin Perdu hosts a series of foodie events and masterclasses. Follow the team on socials or check the website to find out what's coming up.

Chef **Tom Hill** | 3-course dinner from **£40** | Seats **34**
levinperdu.co.uk | 11 West Street, Ashburton, Devon, TQ13 7DT | **01626 927234**

42 Bovey Castle

Historical opulence

From the sweeping driveway leading to this neo-Elizabethan manor house to the warm welcome from tweed-clad porters, a visit to award-winning Bovey Castle always starts in style.

The impressive venue is set on the edge of Dartmoor within 275 acres of lush countryside, where guests can indulge in an array of traditional English country pursuits – from clay pigeon shooting and off-road driving to fly fishing and falconry. There's also an 18-hole championship golf course, along with an all-weather driving range and short-game practice area.

After an action-packed day of activities (or a more leisurely stint of pampering in the Elan Spa), the three-AA-rosette Great Western Grill awaits. Here, head chef Mark Budd puts a modern spin on classic dishes such as fillet of Dartmoor beef wellington with madeira wine sauce and fondant potatoes. Or take a trip to the coast with a salad of native lobster and heritage tomatoes with basil mayonnaise and violet potatoes.

The chef makes the most of the estate's abundant produce, which includes seasonal vegetables, locally reared beef and game, and produce from the kitchen garden. Even desserts get the homegrown treatment in dishes such as the estate's honey and lavender peach-melba baked alaska.

For a more informal dining experience, visit Bovey Castle's Smith's Brasserie where tapas-style snacks and small plates are served with a Dartmoor backdrop.

Trencherman's tip

Begin the dining adventure in style with an aperitif at the glamorous Champagne Bar.

Chef **Mark Budd** | 3-course dinner from **£55** | Seats **70** | Bedrooms **60 plus 22 lodges**
Room rate from **£239** | **EV charging**

boveycastle.com | North Bovey, Devon, TQ13 8RE | **01647 445000**

43 The Chagford Inn

Epic dining on Dartmoor

Visitors to the historical village of Chagford – and they arrive in droves in summer – count themselves lucky if they stumble upon this casual rural inn and discover the excellent eating to be found behind its terracotta facade.

The characterful pub – which received a major interior glow-up this year – is run by chef Ollie Vernon and partner Jordan Ralph (front of house), who serve up astonishingly lovely dining-pub dishes.

The high-quality cooking is rooted in Ollie's commitment to sourcing ingredients direct from farmers who share his values regarding regenerative agriculture and sustainability. Food waste is reduced by whole-carcass butchery done on site.

The restaurant holds an AA rosette but the dining takes place in the laid-back locale of the pub, where locals gather for a pint next to friends feasting on fine food.

Standout dishes on the seasonally changing menu include trotters with pickled walnut on toast – an ode to Ollie's nose-to-tail ethos. There's also a seven-spice Sladesdown duck breast with apricot, watercress and sweet potato, and delish seafood options such as hand-dived Orkney scallop with cauliflower, golden raisins and capers. For a quick and casual lunch, try the homemade corned beef with fried organic egg.

Ollie's desserts are strikingly good: pray the strawberry and Pimm's trifle is on the menu if you visit in summertime.

Trencherman's tip

Book one of the three bedrooms to turn dinner at The Chagford Inn into a foodie break.

Left to right: Ed Hughes of Sharps Brewing Co, Ollie Vernon, Jordan Ralph

Chef **Ollie Vernon** | 3-course dinner from **£30** | Seats **45** | Bedrooms **3** | Room rate from **£70**
thechagfordinn.co.uk | 7 Mill Street, Chagford, Devon, TQ13 8AW | **01647 433109**

44 The Salutation Inn

Smart Topsham dining

Those seeking a culinary interlude en route to Cornwall or yearning for somewhere luxurious to stay on the outskirts of Exeter should book in at this charming restaurant with rooms.

The Salutation Inn has been at the heart of Topsham since 1720 and has a long history of serving patrons as a pub. However, when Tom and Amelia Williams-Hawkes took over in 2012 they transformed it into a refined dining destination.

Over the past decade, the couple have garnered a fantastic reputation for serving some of the best food in the area.

There's a menu to suit every taste and occasion, from the decadent Salutation Supper tasting menu to three-course à la carte and special event dinners. All, however, have a piscatorial leaning (Tom's dad was a salmon fisherman for 30 years and The Salutation has an in-house fishmonger, SALT). Yet they also showcase some of the region's finest meat and veg producers.

Menu items such as a hot seafood platter of oysters, crab, scallops, langoustine, mussels, three species of wild fish, Cornish new potatoes and green salad are composed creatively and presented with flair by head chef Luke Heaver.

Trencherman's tip

While the restaurant space is ideal for an intimate dinner, take lunch or afternoon tea in the GlassHouse: a bright courtyard beneath a glazed atrium with a contemporary botanical vibe.

Chef **Luke Heaver** | 3-course dinner from **£50** | Seats **40** | Bedrooms **6** | Room rate from **£100**
salutationtopsham.co.uk | 68 Fore Street, Topsham, Devon, EX3 0HL | **01392 873060**

45 The Galley Restaurant

Seafood with style

Fresh-from-the-ocean seafood is the calling card of this award-winning restaurant, just a stone's throw from the River Exe.

Located in a charmingly crooked 18th-century townhouse, The Galley has an intimate bistro vibe that makes it an ideal date-night venue. Reserve a table for two and indulge in a couple or three courses from the fish-forward menu – paired with something special from the extensive wine list.

Head chef Louis Huggins majors in bold, clean flavours and regularly updates the line-up to rep the day's catch. Expect to find the likes of scallops with cauliflower, hazelnuts and watercress to start, followed by mains such as pan-roasted hake with kale, Champagne butter sauce and new potatoes.

The carefully curated menu always includes quality meat and vegetarian options too.

The dishes have seen The Galley adorned with an array of accolades including a Michelin plate, a Bib Gourmand and a listing in *Harden's* restaurant guide.

Trencherman's tip

Leave room for the epic cheeseboard of South West dairy favourites such as Kelston Park brie and Pennard Vale goat's cheese.

Chef **Louis Huggins** | 3-course dinner from **£38.50** | Seats **48**
galleyrestaurant.co.uk | 41 Fore Street, Topsham, Devon, EX3 0HU | **01392 876078**

46 The Farm Table at Darts Farm

Next-level plot-to-plate

This restaurant, situated in the food emporium that is Darts Farm, redefines the concept of farm-shop dining.

Food grown on the farm and sourced from local artisan producers is cooked over charcoal or in the wood-fired oven, producing quality dishes that respect the provenance of these exceptional ingredients.

This may be artisan food, but it's not simple: home-reared saddleback pork chops are brined for two days before they hit the pan, while belly pork gets the low-and-slow sous vide treatment before being crisped.

Tom Chivers heads up the open kitchen and revises the menu continuously to reveal what's in its peak micro season. Vibrant veg-centric dishes sit alongside dayboat fish from Brixham and own-reared Red Ruby beef.

For a showstopper, plump for the sharing dish of whole grilled turbot. It's inspired by the Basque ciderhouse tradition of grilling the

fish whole (basted in quality olive oil, vinegar and stock) over fire. Puddings often feature single-origin cacao – crafted by the in-house chocolatiers – and homemade gelato churned from organic milk.

The space comes into its own in the evening, when the rustic decor and setting adjacent to the in-house wine cellar and small-batch cidery lend it a vineyard-restaurant vibe. Explore the wines from Darts' Pebblebed Vineyard (alongside a well-curated list from other wineries), or go off-piste and match dishes with unusual ciders and ales.

Trencherman's tip

A stop at The Farm Table (just five minutes off the M5 near Exeter) is de rigueur on any journey through the South West.

Left to right: Callum Skinner and Han Wang of The Farm Table, James Lloyd of Churchill

Chef **Tom Chivers** | 3-course dinner from **£35** | Seats **70** | **EV charging**

dartsfarm.co.uk | Darts Farm, Topsham, Exeter, Devon, EX3 0QH | **01392 878211**

47 Lympstone Manor

Glamorous star quality

Having cemented its status as the epitome of comfort, exclusivity and luxury, Michael Caines' modern take on the country house hotel continues to dazzle.

Lympstone Manor's star status remains steadfast, having been awarded five AA rosettes, two prestigious Michelin Keys, a Michelin star and an AA Notable Wine List Award, plus being named on La Liste World's Best Restaurants.

Chef-owner Michael and his kitchen brigade craft tasting and à la carte menus loaded with local flavours from land and sea. Immaculately plated dishes include the likes of chicken and truffle mousseline with Wye Valley asparagus, Scottish girolles and Madeira cream sauce. Dine in one of three exquisite rooms named after views across the estuary: Powderham, Mamhead and Berry Head.

The experience is incomplete without sampling artfully matched sips from the Manor's world-class cellar. The list includes award-winning wines such as a Classic Cuvée and Triassic Pinot Noir from Lympstone's own 11-acre vineyard.

Beyond spectacular dining there are numerous other delights, such as a stay in a beautiful room, suite or shepherd's hut, a game of tennis or a wander through the sculpture garden.

Trencherman's tip

Take a dip in the outdoor pool, with its views across the vineyard and the Exe Estuary, before a casual bite to eat at the Pool House Restaurant and Bar.

Chef **Michael Caines MBE** | 3-course lunch from **£75** | Seats **60** | Bedrooms and shepherd's huts **27**
Room rate from **£440** | **EV charging**
lympstonemanor.co.uk | Courtlands Lane, Exmouth, Devon, EX8 3NZ | 01395 202040

48 The Tytherleigh Arms

Hidden hotspot

This 16th-century former coaching inn has sated guests for over 500 years with fine food, drink and hospitality. Since 2011, Mark and Rosie Starling have been at the helm, treating diners to a quality experience that's earned them two AA rosettes, a Michelin Plate, and a spot in the *Good Food Guide*.

Lying in bucolic countryside bordering Devon, Dorset and Somerset, just 20 minutes from the Jurassic Coast, The Tytherleigh Arms is a cracking find. Its cosy and laid-back atmosphere is the perfect setting in which to enjoy the creative dishes pouring from the kitchen.

The culinary team is headed up by chef Nick Topham, who draws out bold yet balanced flavours from seasonal, local produce. Pair this with his eye for detail and discover dishes that are as Instagrammable as they are delicious.

A standout starter pairs cured rainbow trout with tomato jelly, preserved lemon puree, crispy capers and dill mayo. For a sweet finale, lemon verbena set custard, served with poached cherries, almond streusel and refreshing cherry granita, is a great choice among a line-up of tempting puds.

Choose your dining experience: long and lazy Sunday lunch, date-night dinner from the à la carte menu or tasting menu, or overnight stay complete with breakfast. Whichever you opt for, every detail comes with a guarantee of quality, comfort and care.

Trencherman's tip

Opt for the lighter lunch option between Wednesday and Saturday. Smaller dishes, such as tomato arancini or cod goujons with curry sauce, are best paired with a cold drink and shared among friends.

Chef **Nick Topham** | 3-course dinner from **£43** | Seats **56** | Bedrooms **6** | Room rate from **£135** | **EV charging**
tytherleigharms.com | Tytherleigh, Axminster, Devon, EX13 7BE | **01460 220214**

49 The Farmers Arms

Handcrafted to the core

Imagine the dream dining pub: a creative chef crafting sublime dishes; its own farm supplying the homegrown, reared and foraged produce; and an innovative drinks line-up utilising handcrafted cordials and own-infused spirits. And it's all complemented by accommodation that mixes vintage glamour with modern luxury.

A visit to The Farmers Arms (part of The Collective at Woolsery, a curation of village enterprises from tech entrepreneurs Michael and Xochi Birch) turns this wishlist into reality.

Dine in any of the three beautifully rustic dining rooms or bag a table in the garden courtyard to feast alfresco on head chef Toby Neal's reinterpretations of British classics.

The Birch Farm tasting menu provides a seasonal showcase of the produce and meat from The Collective's 150-acre farm and surrounding producers. Delights include the likes of 'Ramson', a main comprising Whiteface Dartmoor hogget with morel and asparagus, and 'Gorse', a pudding of sweet cicely, woodruff and cultured yogurt.

Visiting for a special occasion? The Potting Shed is a delightful spot for up to 18 people to enjoy a private dining experience – complete with seasonal bar and stunning farm location.

On Sundays, plump for a family-style lunch to gorge on a waistband-stretching smorgasbord of roast favourites.

Trencherman's tip

The Collective's accommodation holds a prestigious Michelin Key. Stay in one of the gorgeous suites or rooms above the village shop or push the boat out with a few nights in one of three luxe cottages.

Chef **Toby Neal** | 3-course dinner from **£35** | Seats **50** | Bedrooms **7** | Room rate from **£275**
woolsery.com | Woolsery, Devon, EX39 5QS | **01237 439328**

50 Number Eight

Global fusion

As stalwarts of the Cornish hospitality scene, Joshua Jones and Chloe Wilks had a wealth of industry experience to draw on when, in 2017, they crossed the border to launch their own restaurant in north Devon.

A slew of accolades – including Best Restaurant at the Trencherman's Awards 2021 and Best Restaurant in the Food Reader Awards 2020 – followed and cemented Number Eight's reputation as one of the region's most exciting places to dine. Since those pioneering days, Joshua's continuously evolving tasting menus have garnered a loyal following of foodies from across the region.

The kitchen at this intimate quayside restaurant is a solo operation, with Joshua carefully sourcing top-notch produce for global-fusion dishes. Expect an epic snack selection to start, including the single year-round menu staple of a flavour-popping loaded popadom.

Seafood – in dishes such as wild bass served with roast chicken, wild garlic and mushroom – is sourced from the nearby coastal village of Appledore.

Pre-desserts like lemon sherbet with fennel and white choc add light and shade to the deliciously varied line-up.

Chloe is the friendly face out front who looks after diners with warmth and calm efficiency. To fully enjoy the convivial atmosphere, arrive early for cocktails in the garden or a pre-dinner tipple next to the log burner.

Trencherman's tip

There's no online booking system; Chloe likes to deal with customers on a personal level via an old-school phone call or email.

Chef **Joshua Jones** | Tasting menu from **£85** | Seats **18**

numbereightrestaurant.com | 49 Torrington Street, Bideford, Devon, EX39 4DP | **01237 237589**

51 Sandy Cove Hotel

Spectacular dining in an unrivalled location

When it comes to spectacular dining settings, The Seacliff Restaurant at Sandy Cove Hotel delivers. The intimate venue, which has three AA rosettes and a Michelin listing, clings to a north Devon cliffside between the rolling hills of Exmoor and the raw expanse of the Atlantic.

In this salty-aired setting, head chef Jake Bawn and sous chef Phoenix De-Giorgi craft vibrantly seasonal dishes, with a special focus on seafood. One piscatorial example takes pan-seared scallop and pairs it with bacon jam, white wine foam, and a pop of colour and peppery kick from nasturtium.

The innovative six-course tasting menu blends traditional cooking techniques with modern flavours and precise presentation. It's equally delicious for a leisurely lunch after a coastal crawl as it is for a sunset dinner. Extend the experience and savour the setting with an aperitif or digestif on the outdoor terrace, which overlooks the ocean.

Light-filled rooms (many featuring private sea-view balconies), along with an indoor pool, sauna and steam room, make an indulgent retreat nigh on irresistible. Dog owner? There are designated pet-friendly rooms and easy access to beach walks.

Trencherman's tip

A 20-minute trek down a dirt track takes you to Broadsands Beach, a sheltered cove and one of the best swimming spots on this coastline.

Chefs **Jake Bawn and Phoenix De-Giorgi** | 3-course dinner from **£60** | Seats **30** | Bedrooms **38** Room rate from **£160** | **EV charging**

sandycove-hotel.co.uk | Old Coast Road, Berrynarbor, Ilfracombe, Devon, EX34 9SR | **01271 882243**

52 Restaurant Kensington

Feelgood feasting on Exmoor

Lynton's most exciting new culinary addition mixes up steak suppers with fine fish dishes and smart puds for a deliciously fun night out on Exmoor.

First, those steaks. Exmoor-reared beef is showcased in a top-drawer menu featuring unusual sharing cuts such as chateaubriand, tomahawk and porterhouse, as well as the more commonly found fillet, rump and sirloin.

The beef is treated with reverence by head chef Matthew Rutter and paired with a plethora of sauces and sides like buttery smoked mash, beef-fat carrots and bacon-jam mac and cheese. Indeed, there's such an array of sides and sauces that, even if you chose steak each time you visited, it would take quite some time to feel you'd fully "done" the menu.

However, whether you go full Exmoor farmer with a porterhouse or choose a beautifully cooked piece of fish, it would be remiss not to kick off dinner with a beef-shin croquette or to fail to leave room for pud.

The desserts are particularly beautiful; the chocolate delice is recommended for its malty homemade ice cream, suck-it-off-the-spoon-smooth cocoa delice and crisp shard of praline.

Trencherman's tip

This is the home of the most pimped affogato in the South West: a joyful amalgam of homemade vanilla gelato, coffee brownie, olive-oil roasted almonds, PX sherry, waste-coffee caramel and coffee Italian meringue.

Chef **Matthew Rutter** | 3-course dinner from **£45** | Seats **35**
restaurantkensington.co.uk | 1 Castle Hill, Lynton, Devon, EX35 6JA | **07467 411585**

Steeped in history. Made with
passion. Perfected by science.

trevethandistillery.com

TREVETHAN

SINCE 1929

53 The Castle Inn, Lydford

Moorland magnetism

The Castle Inn, with its cosiness, comfort food and moorland magnetism, is a real foodie find. Hannah and Jared Lothian are the heart and soul of this 16th-century pub, found in a fairytale setting amid wooded valleys close to the Granite Way trail.

Determined to reinvigorate the ancient building and turn it into a welcoming community hub, the couple took it on as tenants in 2019 and have since brought home a haul of awards – a sure sign of its new-chapter success.

The menu hits the crowd-pleasing sweet spot where elevated pub classics meet fancier fare. Whipping up the goods in the kitchen is award-winning chef Mike Palmer (best known for his long tenure at nearby Two Bridges Hotel in Princetown), whose cooking creds make him a bewitching addition to this pub.

Mike majors on fulsome flavours, so expect starters such as torched peach, ripped burrata and hot honey. Mains are equally packed with flavour and texture and include the likes of Holsworthy pork tenderloin with bubble and squeak, confit fennel and cider café au lait. Pimped-up desserts include banoffee mousse with caramel crème and chocolate crumb.

As a guarantee of ingredient origin, the menu lists the vast range of local suppliers.

Trencherman's tip

Hannah and Jared also run The Copley Arms in Cornwall. Visit for similar community-centric values, warm hospitality and fab food on the River Seaton, just five minutes from the sea.

Chef **Mike Palmer** | 3-course dinner from **£32** | Seats **75** | Bedrooms **13** | Room rate from **£130**
castleinnlydford.co.uk | Lydford, Okehampton, Devon, EX20 4BH | **01822 820242**

54 The Fig Tree @ 36

Parisian flavours in Plymouth

This charming family bistro near Royal William Yard enjoys a sterling reputation with locals and visitors alike.

Head chef Ryan Marsland's dishes are a celebration of Devon's fruitful land and sea, including compilations like beef cheek arancini with roast tomato sauce, parmesan and onion; and Cornish pork belly with brown-butter potato terrine.

The line-up changes daily, but guests will discover a leaning towards French cooking in the likes of fish stew packed with local pollock, monkfish, mussels, whiting and langoustine, served with potatoes, greens and roast garlic aioli.

A keenly priced lunch menu and a Trust the Chef menu on Wednesday and Thursday are fabulous ways to delve into The Fig Tree experience – the latter removing the decision fatigue that's so often the by-product of a tempting menu.

If the forecast is favourable, book one of the tables under the fig tree in the garden and kick off an alfresco supper with cocktails, plump olives and homemade bread. The restaurant is tucked away on a residential street a short walk from Royal William Yard and perfect for a post-lunch stroll along the harbour.

Trencherman's tip

A takeaway menu, available day and night, offers indulgent delights including focaccia sandwiches, mussels and risotto.

Chef **Ryan Marsland** | 3-course dinner from **£45** | Seats **40**
figtree36.co.uk | 36 Admiralty Street, Stonehouse, Plymouth, Devon, PL1 3RU | **01752 253247**

55 Salumi Bar & Eatery

Smorgasbord of dining delights

Salumi has established itself as a go-to spot for Plymouth residents, thanks to its flexible dining approach and ultra-friendly service. Whether it's a Sunday lunch, date-night dinner or cocktails and a sharing board with friends, all bases are covered.

Inside, turquoise-painted tables, chairs and fittings contrast with oak beams and exposed brick walls to create a rustic-cool vibe. Seating is split across multiple levels, plus there's the opportunity to dine alfresco in Salumi's Garden of Dreams – a large outdoor courtyard area with wooden benches and a fire kitchen, where many of the dishes are prepared.

Chefs Dave Jenkins and Jake Hardington have created menus to suit any whim, be it full-blown feasting or nibbles over drinks. Dishes such as black bream with St Austell Bay mussels, thai butter sauce, spiced jersey royals, sumac and yogurt sit next to casual steak burgers.

Additional carnivorous highlights on the à la carte menu include Dartmoor lamb rump with courgette and aubergine puree, and pork chop served with 'nduja croquette, salsa verde, crackling and chips.

The food is modern British, encompassing flavours from across the globe and unconstrained by tradition. Take the super-popular Sunday lunch menu, featuring classic roasts alongside small plates such as bao bun with barbecued king oyster mushroom, soy, sesame and chilli.

Look out for tasty pop-up events such as curry and cocktail or taco and tequila evenings.

Trencherman's tip

Order a round of frozen margs for your gang. A newly installed slushy machine at Salumi takes the favourite cocktail next-level.

Chefs **Dave Jenkins and Jake Hardington** | 3-course dinner from **£35** | Seats **50**
eatsalumi.co.uk | 18 Millbay Road, Plymouth, Devon, PL1 3LH | **01752 267538**

56 Gara Rock

Laid-back coastal luxury

Head down winding rural lanes in lush, coastal south Devon to discover Gara Rock, a destination hotel with a stunning clifftop restaurant serving smart seasonal dishes and more laid-back fare.

Floor-to-ceiling windows showcase unrivalled views of the waves below, making this a feast for the eyes as well as the belly.

At Restaurant at Gara, the focus is on locally sourced seafood from Devon and Cornwall, expertly prepared and ultra fresh. Delicacies such as Cornish red mullet with wild garlic chimichurri are elevated by seasonal ingredients sourced from the hotel's kitchen garden.

For casual all-day options, Kitchen at Gara (the pooch-friendly half of the restaurant) offers crowd-pleasers such as pork and apple scotch egg with piccalilli, while Terrace at Gara specialises in hand-stretched sourdough pizzas. The Picante comes with

Cobble Lane 'nduja, rocket, Gara-fermented honey and a side helping of coastal views.

'GaraRoo' is the tongue-in-cheek name for the hotel's in-room takeaway service, giving guests the option to indulge in signature dishes from the comfort of their suite.

Zero-waste practices are also followed, with leftover ingredients used to create inventive concoctions when infused in spirits.

Trencherman's tip

Head to the gin bar to sample the fifth edition of Gara Rock Gin, a collab with small-batch specialist Devon Distillery. It features seriously umami flavours of yuzu, bergamot and passion pepper.

Chef **Paul Hegley** | 3-course dinner from **£55** | Seats **40** | Bedrooms **35** | Room rate from **£109** | **EV charging**
gararock.com | East Portlemouth, near Salcombe, Devon, TQ8 8FA | **01548 845946**

57 The Millbrook Inn

New chapter for popular dining pub

Since the Owens family took over this pub in the pretty village of South Pool in 2021, they've been honing its culinary character. Now, it's gone next-level with the arrival of Elly Wentworth as the pub's exec chef.

Elly most recently headed up The Angel of Dartmouth and has worked at prestigious establishments including Restaurant Hywel Jones at Lucknam Park. She has also represented the South West three times on the BBC's *Great British Menu*.

Elly has incredible produce to work with at the Millbrook, as the pub's sister business Fowlescombe Farm (she also heads up its Refectory restaurant) supplies meat from native and rare British breeds.

Her precise, produce-led approach centres on provenance; the kitchen takes its cue from what's reared on the regeneratively tended land, as well as what's landed on the nearby coast.

At the pub, these ingredients form dishes such as roasted rump of lamb with chargrilled summer vegetables and black olive tapenade, and hearty pork chop with roasted fennel and french mustard sauce.

For ultimate comfort eating, organic grass-fed beef – dry-aged for 45 days and served with chips, greens and peppercorn sauce – is pretty hard to beat.

Trencherman's tip

Stylish guest accommodation at two cottages across the road delivers Egyptian cotton sheets, luxury toiletries and a slap up breakfast in the morning.

Chef **Elly Wentworth** | 3-course dinner from **£48** | Seats **80**
millbrookinnsouthpool.co.uk | South Pool, Kingsbridge, Devon, TQ7 2RW | **01548 531581**

58 The Horse

Casual nosebag on the moor

Dartmoor pubs tend to focus on traditional fodder, but this gem in the market town of Moretonhampstead offers a more unusual dining experience.

Head to the authentic family-run inn for Mediterranean-inspired cooking in a classic pub setting. Chef-owner Nigel Hoyle dishes up a menu majoring on thin-crust, romana-style pizza – but these are a far cry from the usual takeaway variety.

Twice-risen focaccia dough is rolled thinly and piled with locally sourced and Italian-imported artisan ingredients. Crowd-pleasing combos include the 'Vesuvio' ('nduja sausage, chorizo, fresh onions, confit potatoes, buffalo mozzarella and oregano) and 'The Eastern' (spiced lamb, peppers, cumin-roasted onions, harissa and tahini).

Beyond the pizza oven, try dishes such as the Pasta Pollo Pugliese of tarragon chicken meatballs in rich tomato ragout with creamed orecchiette, or white bean and fennel cassoulet with butter-roasted hake, tiger prawns and smoked tomato aioli.

Puds are equally casual but captivating – think homemade rhubarb crumble with custard pannacotta.

The Horse is a great spot to visit with a crowd as its range of antipasti and pizza is made for sharing. And what can't be finished can be taken home in a takeaway container.

Trencherman's tip

After dinner, trot along to one of The Horse's three boutique guest rooms, which come with super-king beds and smart bathrooms.

Chef **Nigel Hoyle** | 3-course dinner from **£22** | Seats **60** | Bedrooms **3** | Room rate from **£120**
thehorsedartmoor.co.uk | 7 George Street, Moretonhampstead, Devon, TQ13 8PG | **01647 440242**

59 Mill End Hotel and Restaurant

Decadent feasting on Dartmoor

This converted 15th-century flour mill, set on the banks of the River Teign, is a multi-award-winning and utterly idyllic spot for lunch, afternoon tea or a candlelit dinner on Dartmoor.

Whether plumping for the daytime Lounge and Lawn menu or visiting for the à la carte line-up, relish the fact that almost every element on the plate has been crafted in-house by head chef William Broom and his kitchen crew. This includes the bread, cakes, sauces and even the bottled water, which is tapped on-site from a deep moorland source before going through a seven-stage filtration and purification process.

Dinner in the two-AA-rosette restaurant is a decadent affair featuring locally landed seafood, South West cheeses, meat from nearby farms and a raft of local suppliers including Devon Venison. Ingredients are fashioned into thoughtful dishes plated with flair.

A taste of what's on offer includes Sladesdown Farm chicken and pork terrine with pickled veg; battered fish du jour with pommes allumettes, buttered hispi cabbage, brown shrimp and tartare sauce; and twice-baked cheese soufflé with forest fungi mushroom, chestnut spinach and black truffle fondue. Take post-dinner drinks in the smart lounge.

In the summer months, bag a table in the lush garden to munch on casual plates such as a ploughman's lunch or a Mill FLT (fish finger, lettuce and tomato) sandwich.

Feeling organised? Restaurant bookings can be taken up to three months in advance.

Trencherman's tip

Mill End has a number of bespoke rooms and suites for guests bringing canine companions. Pampered pooches are waited on hand and paw throughout their stay with welcome packs, breakfast sausages and dedicated dining areas.

Chef **William Broom** | 3-course dinner from **£45** | Seats **43** | Bedrooms **21** | Room rate from **£150** | **EV charging**
millendhotel.com | Chagford, Newton Abbot, Devon, TQ13 8JN | **01647 432282**

60 Harry's Restaurant

Feelgood feasting in the heart of the city

Harry's is a highly unusual find in Exeter city centre. Where the chains have devoured so many indies, Harry's has remained a family-run restaurant and the discerning local's go-to for 30 years.

Samantha Pounds' parents launched Harry's in 1993, and now she and her four daughters man the helm. They craft smart and crowd-pleasing brunches, lunches and dinners in the Victorian Gothic-style building, which once the workshop of 19th-century architectural sculptor Harry Hems.

Start any visit with one of the well-crafted cocktails (the sweet-sharp French 75 is a great shout), before digging into indulgent starters like the famed cheddar soufflé topped with crispy shallots, and the crisp, hot arancini dipped in truffle mayonnaise.

The restaurant's relationship with nearby suppliers reflects their decades in the business. Supporting fellow local indies such as Darts Farm, Godminster and The Sidwell Street Bakehouse is prioritised – and namechecked on the menu.

For mains, choose something light such as Devon crab linguine with chilli, lemon, white wine and cherry tomatoes. Or opt for pure hedonism via quality chateaubriand with a side of marrowbone in garlic crumb. And if the homemade blood-orange and frangipane tart is on the dessert menu, don't hesitate.

Trencherman's tip

Harry's is all about the good times and is a perfect spot for a sociable dinner with the gang.

Chef **Samantha Pounds** | 3-course dinner from **£45** | Seats **62**
harrysrestaurants.co.uk | 86 Longbrook Street, Exeter, Devon, EX4 6AP | **01392 202234**

61 The View Restaurant

Family spirit in a hotel setting

This restaurant on the eighth floor of Courtyard by Marriott at Sandy Park is breaking the hotel-dining mould, having cultivated a family-run restaurant vibe in its sleek penthouse location.

Chef Matt Mason (dad) crafts the beautiful food for which he's long been recognised in the area. Joanne (mum) runs front of house as senior maitre d' and restaurant manager/sommelier Charlie (son) impresses with his wine knowledge. The experience combines warm hospitality with a distinct passion for Devon's quality produce.

Matt is the driving force behind the vision. The chef has long had a fan club of foodies – garnered from his 25-year tenure at The Jack in the Green and chef-director stint at Winslade Manor. However, this new venture with the rest of the Mason clan could be his most pivotal yet.

A concise three-course menu reveals refined dishes that reflect Matt's experienced hand and the long-established relationships he's nurtured with local producers and suppliers of note.

Roast monkfish tail, rack of local lamb with orzo pasta, and slow-braised pork belly with pickled kohlrabi are all standout creations on the attractive menu. In the mood for something more casual? A Mibrasa charcoal-grill menu delivers quality dry-aged steaks cooked over flame.

Trencherman's tip

The M5 beneath you fades into insignificance amid the vast panorama of lush countryside that rolls out beyond it. Arrive early to soak up the views from the bar area. The slick spot has low sofas beside vast windows – the perfect space for lounging with an aperitif.

Chef **Matthew Mason** | 3-course dinner from **£45** | Seats **150**

theviewexeter.co.uk | Courtyard by Marriott 8th floor, Sandy Park Way, Exeter, Devon, EX2 7NN | **01392 576677**

Speciality foods for restaurants
and retailers, produced and
delivered with passion and expertise
for 45 years

harveyandbrockless.co.uk

HARVEY & BROCKLESS
the fine food co

62 Saveur

European inspo in Exmouth

There's no need to cross the Channel to experience Parisian bistro vibes when a seaside excursion to Exmouth reveals a vraiment délicieux dining encounter.

Hidden away on a pedestrianised street just off the main square, Saveur is where chef-patron Nigel Wright works solo in the kitchen, crafting modern, seasonal dishes of two-AA-rosette status.

Nigel's excellent menus celebrate all things local and seasonal and lean towards seafood thanks to the venue's proximity to the ocean – and Nigel's hotline to the fishmongers at Brixham Fish Market. A starter of monkfish scampi with sweetcorn salsa and curry oil can be chased by the catch of the day – typically served with romesco sauce or salsa verde – for diners who want to experience the dayboats' freshest haul.

For those less piscatorially inclined, the options are just as delicious. Seasonal examples include Powderham fillet steak with bone marrow mash, confit garlic, braised beef cheek and truffle sauce.

Conclude proceedings with a cheeseboard stacked with fine fromage including Twanger Cheddar from Green's of Glastonbury, Wyfe of Bath from The Bath Soft Cheese Co., and Driftwood from White Lake Cheese.

The service is as laid-back and welcoming as the decor, making this a charming find for a casual lunch with friends or an intimate dinner à deux.

Trencherman's tip

Want to make the most of the restrained but impressive wine list? Saveur is just a 30-minute train ride from Exeter.

Chef **Nigel Wright** | 3-course dinner from **£45** | Seats **25**
saveursrestaurant.com | 9 Tower Street, Exmouth, Devon, EX8 1NT | **01395 269459**

63 Restaurant 1685 at Colcombe Castle Hotel

Fresh and fancy

Every boutique hotel needs a sidekick stellar restaurant to help lure discerning diners. Restaurant 1685 by chef-patron Chris Chatfield is just that, having cranked up the dining credentials of restyled Colcombe Castle Hotel in east Devon.

Chris sharpened his culinary skills at notable South West dining destinations including The Horn of Plenty, Alexandra Hotel and Winslade Manor, before embarking on this new venture in Colyton.

Located in a pretty patch of Devonshire countryside near the Jurassic Coast, the boutique hotel continues the pleasing aesthetics inside thanks to a recent refurb. The restaurant's vaulted ceilings, attractive tableware and inviting hues of copper, sea blues and greens create a polished vibe, which is matched by the food served.

Chris's commitment to sourcing local ingredients and forging long-lasting relationships with nearby growers and fishermen is documented in smart à la carte and tasting menus brimful of fresh produce.

The restaurant is open three nights a week, so it's worth scheduling a trip accordingly to sample the confident cooking with thoughtful flavour combinations. Warm up with Lyme Bay scallops dressed in mango, curry, coriander and Oscietra caviar, before delving into venison loin with fermented blackberries, tarragon, black-pudding brioche and cocoa jus.

Trencherman's tip

Time for an aperitif? Imbibe a local ale or cider, or explore the globetrotting wine list at the relaxing lounge bar.

Chef **Chris Chatfield** | 3-course dinner from **£60** | Seats **38** | Bedrooms **6** | Room rate from **£130**
colcombecastle.co.uk | Market Place, Colyton, Devon, EX24 6JS | **01297 529251**

64 Watersmeet Hotel

Coastal cuisine

Watersmeet Hotel, awarded Condé Nast Johansens Best Waterside Hotel 2024, is an intimate boutique escape framed by breathtaking sea views across the north Devon coast. Guests also enjoy direct, private access to the pristine sands of Combesgate, so it's a hotspot for beach lovers.

Inside, a smart refurb has seen Rocks Restaurant, Palms Room (the hotel's informal bistro) and other areas enjoy a glow-up with New England-inspired decor. The chic and tranquil aesthetic feels contemporary and airy with its Lloyd Loom chairs and wooden flooring.

Rocks Restaurant presents a thoughtfully curated and seasonally evolving menu, which has earned the venue two AA rosettes. Born and bred in nearby Barnstaple, head chef John Cairns is devoted to championing local produce.

Dishes such as pan-fried scallops with celeriac puree, and venison loin with pickled plums, can be relished alongside an extensive wine list and sweeping sea views.

Dining is open to all – hotel guests or not – so anyone is welcome to drop by for a light lunch or afternoon tea, or book in for a lavish evening meal. Hotel residents, however, can also enjoy indoor and outdoor heated pools, luxurious spa facilities and bespoke treatments, so it's worth making it a weekender.

Trencherman's tip

On Saturdays, hotel guests gather on the lawn to offer a gentle namaste to the day. There's nothing quite like a soothing yoga session with a soundtrack of crashing waves to start the day right.

Chef **John Cairns** | 3-course dinner from **£65** | Seats **55** | Bedrooms **27** | Room rate from **£200** | **EV charging**
watersmeethotel.co.uk | The Esplanade, Woolacombe, Devon, EX34 7EB | **01271 870333**

Dorset

Dorset

Numbers on the map correspond to the numbers next to the restaurants in the guide.

70 WAREHAM

73
BOURNEMOUTH

Locations are approximate

65 Three Horseshoes Pub & Kitchen

Asian-inspired seafood thrills

This 300-year-old thatched pub, in the village of Burton Bradstock on the Jurassic Coast, delivers quality cooking and a refreshingly unpretentious vibe.

Husband-and-wife team Jaap and Hannah Schep met while working for the Marriott group and now delight diners with their own take on hospitality.

A good proportion of the menu majors on local fish, and Dutch-born chef Jaap is especially fond of pan-Asian flavour profiles. Indonesian seafood curry of monkfish cheek, tiger prawns, and mussels, served with basmati rice and soy-steamed greens, sits comfortably alongside more British-leaning pub dishes like the Chesil Smokery seafood ploughman's.

Visitors should also check out the pub's alluring selection of bar snacks which, in quantity, could kick plans for a starter, main and pud into touch. Who wouldn't enjoy working their way through small plates of cockle popcorn, Portland Pearl oysters and bluefin tuna tostada with avocado, lime, soy, chilli, cucumber, sesame and coriander?

There's a substantial list of by-the-bottle and by-the-glass wines, and the menu includes many English sparkling wines and intriguing international finds.

Trencherman's tip

Full table service is available in the garden, so outdoor diners receive the same excellent experience as those dining indoors. Go alfresco on a sunny Sunday for a roast lunch showcasing slow-cooked local meats.

Chef **Jaap Schep** | 3-course dinner from **£32** | Seats **65**

threehorseshoesburtonbradstock.co.uk | Mill Street, Burton Bradstock, Dorset, DT6 4QZ | **01308 897259**

66 Brassica Restaurant

Design-led dining

Having run a series of successful restaurants in London, chef Cass Titcombe relocated to Dorset with his partner, designer Louise Chidgey, in 2014 to establish a business that would blend their skills and passions. The result? A design-led, family-run restaurant putting provenance front and centre.

Cass's modern European cooking combines local produce with specialist ingredients, plus influences from Spain and Italy, to create dishes that sing with flavour.

The menu changes daily depending on what the kitchen team can get their hands on, as they endeavour to source all fresh ingredients from within 15 miles of the restaurant. They're also committed to serving organic meat and dairy, alongside dayboat fish and Dorset-grown veg.

Breakfast, brunch and lunch menus extend the dining opportunities. Try the likes of cavatelli with roasted aubergines, courgettes, green beans and olives or whole grilled crevettes with garlic, chilli and parsley butter.

The Brassica family has grown since 2014. Adjacent to the restaurant is lifestyle store Brassica Mercantile, a veritable treasure trove of delicious edibles and homewares. Then there's Brassica Forno in Bridport, which is a bakery, shop and production kitchen. It's here that the team also produce their award-winning Brassica Handmade ready meals.

Trencherman's tip

Aperitivo Hour, between 6 and 7pm on Friday and Saturday, offers well-priced cocktails and complimentary small plates.

Chef **Cass Titcombe** | 3-course dinner from **£40** | Seats **38**
brassica.uk | 4 The Square, Beaminster, Dorset, DT8 3AS | **01308 538100**

67 The Acorn Inn

Dine in Hardy country

Mentioned in *Tess of the d'Urbervilles* and located near the birthplace of its author Thomas Hardy, The Acorn delivers everything you'd expect of a history-steeped English coaching inn.

Exposed beams, oak-panelled walls and roaring log fires all reference its 16th-century origins. However, it's the award-winning, two-AA-rosette restaurant that attracts a contemporary clientele, thanks to chef Ana Martins' seasonally changing menus, which capitalise on Dorset's finest produce.

The bounty of the coast and countryside – and the restaurant's own veggie and herb garden – can be discovered in refreshingly unpretentious dishes. A Jurassic Coast duo of pork belly and shoulder, for example, is partnered with sous-vide swede, charred shallots, purple carrot and vermouth jus. Veggie and vegan diners are

well catered for via a growing number of options incorporating fungi, grains and spices.

Epic puds, such as a deconstructed rhubarb and custard confection with sweet shortcrust pastry and rhubarb gelato, complete the proceedings.

Book a bed for the night to get the full coaching inn experience – and the opportunity to explore the expansive drinks list. The cocktail line-up namechecks South West spirits including Conker Gin, Black Cow Vodka and Devon Rum Co., while local wines come courtesy of West Dorset's Furleigh Estate.

Trencherman's tip

The light bites menu changes monthly and includes delights such as king prawn brioche toast with Kewpie mayo and caviar, and lamb koftas with chimichurri and tzatziki.

Chef **Ana Martins** | 3-course dinner from **£45** | Seats **40** | Bedrooms **10** | Room rate from **£150**
acorn-inn.co.uk | 28 Fore Street, Evershot, Dorset, DT2 0JW | **01935 83228**

68 Crab House Cafe

Seafood and sustainability

Overlooking Dorset's famed Chesil Beach, Crab House Cafe is a rustic, laid-back spot where visitors can feast on seafood plucked from the ocean mere metres away.

Sustainability is paramount here. Owner Nigel Bloxham works closely with local fishermen to source seafood from the surrounding waters – which is usually served the day it's caught. Crab remoulade (handpicked Portland white claw meat, celeriac, dijon mustard, Isle of Wight tomato virgin bloody mary gel, cucumber and apple) or roasted rack of brill with marsh samphire and hollandaise sauce provide a glimpse of the dishes to be discovered on the ever-changing menu.

The cafe's eponymous crustacean is arguably best enjoyed à deux. Whole Portland brown crab is served in signature style with dressed salad and mayo. Those who enjoy flame-fired fish should opt for skewers of marinated monkfish and gurnard – roasted over coals – with red lentil and yogurt tikka-masala-style curry, preserved lemon and coriander rice, poppadom and yogurt dip.

Arguably the stars of the show are the oysters. Grown at the cafe's oyster farm just a short paddle from the restaurant, the prized bivalves are fresh, plump and best slurped au naturel.

Trencherman's tip

Pair the seafood with your pick of an extensive wine list, which includes bottles from Bridport's Furleigh Estate, or a locally brewed Crab House Mussel Ale or Oyster Stout.

Chef **George Brace** | 3-course dinner from **£40** | Seats **43**

crabhousecafe.co.uk | Ferrymans Way, Portland Road, Wyke Regis, Dorset, DT4 9YU | **01305 788867**

69 Catch at the Old Fish Market

Next chapter for seafood favourite

Built in 1855 using local Portland stone, Weymouth's Grade II-listed Old Fish Market provides a fitting home for a restaurant delivering sustainable sea-to-plate dining.

The restaurant is now in the capable hands of chef-patron Ben Champkin, who brings a wealth of top-drawer kitchen experience to the proceedings. Former head chef at The Newt in Somerset and sous chef at L'Enclume in the Lake District, the Dorset-raised chef has a culinary philosophy of utilising the finest local ingredients with simplicity and precision.

It's no surprise, then, that Catch serves the freshest fish and shellfish drawn from clear Dorset waters. Savour it while overlooking the harbour and basking in the light flooding through the clerestory windows.

Each dish is a celebration of Weymouth's coastal flavours and a culinary journey through its rich maritime history. Line-caught sea bass is elevated to star status with the assistance of wild garlic, asparagus, cockle vinegar and smoked roe, while Portland crab with accompaniments of hollandaise and broth shows off the fresh shellfish without any unnecessary fripperies.

Downstairs you'll find traditional fishmonger Weyfish. Arrive at the right time to see dayboats landing baskets of Portland crab and lobster, line-caught sea bass, mackerel and pollock.

Trencherman's tip

Book for lunch to enjoy a relaxed coastal feast highlighting the season's best regional ingredients, cooked with care over Dorset charcoal in a Josper oven. The experience begins and ends with individually plated dishes, while the main course is served for sharing.

Chef **Ben Champkin** | 4-course dinner from **£65** | Seats **42**

catchattheoldfishmarket.com | 1 Custom House Quay, Weymouth, Dorset, DT4 8BE | 01305 590555

70 The Garden Room at The Priory

Ancient monastery turned boutique bolthole

There aren't many ancient country house hotels tucked away down a stone-walled alleyway just off a bustling high street, so The Priory is a rather unusual find.

Push open the heavy wooden door to discover a Grade II*-listed building set in four acres of English cottage gardens and overlooking the banks of the River Frome. Expect old stonework, hidden archways and unique architectural features at every turn. To describe it as idyllic would be an understatement.

There's evidence of a dwelling at the site from as early as 809, and it has been a nunnery, monastery and private home in its former guises. The decor has been kept delightfully traditional to honour this heritage, a theme running through each of the individually furnished guest rooms of the main house. Additional accommodation can be found in the renovated 16th-century Boat House.

A bold concession to modernity, The Garden Room restaurant is a glass-walled, green-oak-beamed dining room overlooking manicured lawns and riverbank.

Here, head chef Stephan Guinebault distracts guests from the views by transforming impeccably sourced produce into classics such as mint-crusted rack of lamb with truffle pommes anna, char rhubarb and celery, roscoff onion soubise and a lamb and olive oil jus. For a treat-yourself dinner, the rosemary-roasted Dorset 'Devon Red' chateaubriand is knockout.

Trencherman's tip

The Priory offers a reduced same-day-arrival rate for spontaneous nights away.

Chef **Stephan Guinebault** | 3-course dinner from **£80** | Seats **56** | Bedrooms **17** | Room rate from **£230** | **EV charging**
theprioryhotel.co.uk | Church Green, Wareham, Dorset, BH20 4ND | **01929 551666**

71 Tom's Lyme Regis

Seafood scoffing on the harbour

Coastal resorts don't come much prettier than Lyme Regis, with its picturesque promenade overlooking the historic Cobb. Tom's Lyme Regis has a coveted spot just a stone's throw from the water, so the boat-to-plate journey of its sought-after seafood is a matter of yards.

Lyme Bay scallops, prawns and crab vie for top billing on a seafood-laden menu that often features fresh oysters and Dorset Blue lobster. However, the pièce de résistance on the line-up is Tom's Fish Board, which features thrills like pan-roasted Lyme Bay scallops with burnt lime and sriracha butter and roast monkfish.

On balmy days, laze on the oceanfront terrace with a glass of fizz from nearby Castlewood Vineyard while enjoying a bite from the lunch menu – the Lyme Bay lobster roll doesn't disappoint.

Drop in on a Friday or Saturday between 5pm and 6pm to delight in Portland Pearl Oyster and Cocktail happy hour.

There are options for both meat eaters and vegetarians at Tom's, but it's really the seafood that's the main draw, with a bill that changes daily to reflect the day's catch. Indeed, it's not unusual for Tom to take delivery of a freshly caught haul in the afternoon and work it into that evening's menu.

Trencherman's tip

Start the day as you mean to go on with a farmhouse-style breakfast at the restaurant. It's served every day between 9.45am and 11am and includes classic dishes like hot-smoked salmon and scrambled eggs on sourdough.

Chef **Tom Robinson** | 3-course dinner from **£37** | Seats **28**
tomslymeregis.com | Marine Parade, Lyme Regis, Dorset, DT7 3JQ | **01297 816018**

72 The Ilchester Arms

Dorset's delicious new dining pub

Chef Paul Brinicombe and his partner (and front-of-house pro) Ariana Ruth have turned a 16th-century pub in the quaint village of Symondsbury into something rather special.

The thatched pub's reinvention centres around locally sourced, pared-back, ingredient-driven food, on a menu that's chalked up on the wall and where dishes are gratifyingly crossed off when sold out.

Tables in the casual dining room are furnished with white tablecloths, crisp cotton napkins, unfussy cutlery and miniature coloured vases filled with fresh cottage flowers. It's a makeover that's grid-friendly and authentic in equal measure.

Chef-owner Paul (whose CV includes a stint as head chef at the Royal Clarence Hotel) traces his culinary inspiration back to a childhood spent in his grandfather's veg patch and watching his grandmother pickling produce. It's little surprise, then, that his dishes have a field-to-fork vibe, as well as a contemporary edge that keeps the compilations exciting.

Cheffed-up pub classics rub along nicely with Paul's more original creations such as whole roast lemon sole, sauce vierge and crispy oysters; Isle of Wight tomato flatbread with white bean hummus and green sauce; and Colmers Ale-brined chicken schnitzel with cabbage slaw and aioli.

Trencherman's tip

The drinks menu is as interesting as the food. A line-up of natural wines features alongside expertly crafted cocktails, designed exclusively for the pub by mixologist supremo Jack Wareing.

Chef **Paul Brinicombe** | 3-course dinner from **£45** | Seats **25**

ilchesterarmssymondsbury.co.uk | Miles Cross, Symondsbury, Bridport, Dorset, DT6 6HD | **01308 422600**

73 Thirteen

Artistic tasting experience

Thirteen is located a short detour from Poole Quay and Sandbanks on Dorset's famed coastline. It's not the street number that lends the intimate restaurant its name, however, but the number of plates on its artistic tasting menu.

There's space for 20 diners, plus two in pole position at the heart of the open kitchen, but while the Parkstone restaurant may be small in scale, it's big in reputation. Featuring in the *Michelin Guide* and with a host of hard-earned accolades under its belt, Thirteen may need a bigger belt soon.

Dishes lean towards modern British, and the steady stream of 13 plates are all masterfully executed, balanced and artfully plated. Discerning diners find food for thought in dishes like India-meets-Jamaica goat samosa and south coast cod with langoustine bisque and cured fennel.

It's a family affair, too. Alex Naik is head chef, his sister, Frances, heads up front of house, and parents, Hem and Elisabeth, bring the wine knowledge. And the final ingredient? A passion for produce – watchwords here are seasonality, sustainability, homegrown, locally sourced, fished and foraged.

Trencherman's tip

Prefer to have half the number of plates? There's a 6½ option on weekdays and lunchtimes. Thirteen also conjures up a memorable roast on selected Sundays.

Chef **Alex Naik** | 3-course dinner from **£115** | Seats **22**

thirteenrestaurant.com | 222 Ashley Road, Parkstone, Poole, Dorset, BH14 9BY | **01202 376635**

Bath, Bristol & Somerset

Bath, Bristol & Somerset

Numbers on the map correspond to the numbers next to the restaurants in the guide.

WESTON-SUPER-MARE

Quantock Hills AONB

74

TAUNTON

75

CHARD

Blackdown Hills AONB

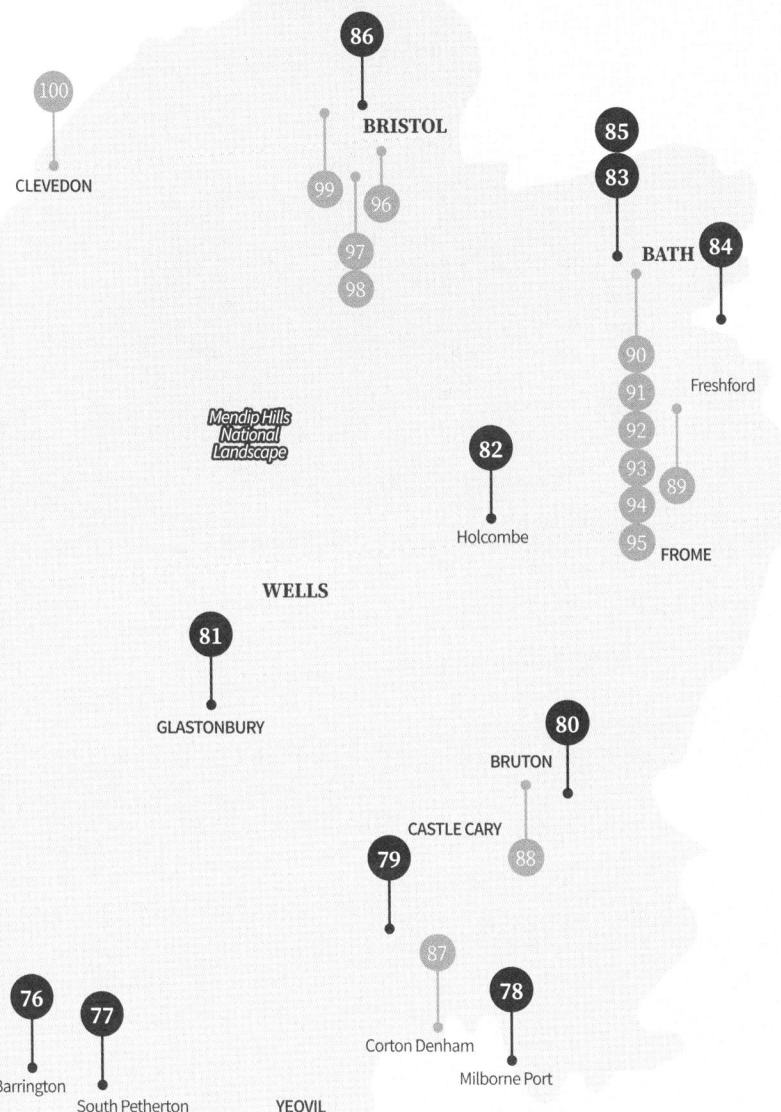

100
CLEVEDON

86
BRISTOL
99
96
97
98

85
83
BATH 84

90
91
92
93
94
95

Freshford
89
FROME

Mendip Hills
National
Landscape

82
Holcombe

WELLS

81
GLASTONBURY

80
BRUTON
88

CASTLE CARY
79

87
Corton Denham

78
Milborne Port

76
Barrington

77
South Petherton

YEOVIL

74 Augustus

Taunton's favourite neighbourhood bistro

This glass-fronted spot is hidden within an intimate courtyard in Taunton's town centre and could easily be missed – were it not for its stellar reputation.

Augustus enjoys a loyal following of foodies who love it for its high-calibre cooking and comfortable decor.

For more than a decade, owners Richard Guest and Cedric Chirrosel have proved that the hallmarks of a consistently good restaurant are top-notch front-of-house service, smart cooking and quality ingredients.

The pair are dedicated supporters of other local indies so just about everything that ends up on the plate is sourced nearby. Fresh fruit and veg come from local growers and suppliers including Granny Smiths, Pitney Farm and Capland Acre, while freshly landed fish is delivered direct from Brixham and meat is sourced from Riverside Butchers.

Richard's cooking style leans towards classic French cuisine while celebrating seasonal British produce. Popular dishes include starters like Devon smoked eel with scrambled egg, herring caviar and curry oil on bread, and mains such as rabbit faggots with gratin potato, mixed greens and a rich onion gravy.

Puds take the shape of British classics, including Yorkshire rhubarb and custard tart with honeycomb.

Trencherman's tip

Observer food critic Jay Rayner described Augustus as *'a classy bistro that will look after you and make the world feel just that little bit better'.*

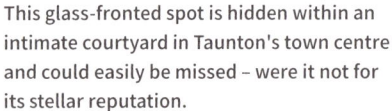

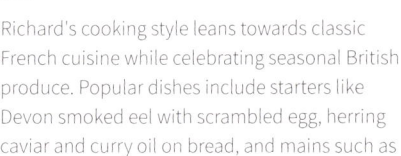

Chef **Richard Guest** | 3-course dinner from **£42** | Seats **40**
augustustaunton.co.uk | 3 The Courtyard, St James Street, Taunton, Somerset, TA1 1JR | **01823 324354**

75 The Cotley Inn

Grade II-listed village pub

An evening on The Cotley Inn's south-facing terrace provides a feast for the senses: bees buzz around lavender, delicious smells emanate from flavourful dishes and visual delight is provided by views of fields where many of the ingredients are grown or reared.

The Grade II-listed country inn sits in the heart of the Cotley Estate in the Blackdown Hills and has been exquisitely updated in contemporary farmhouse style by owners Maddie Beaumont and Ben Porter.

Four country-chic bedrooms accompany the restaurant and make it a delicious location for a stopover. In addition to the sumptuous feasting, guests can look forward to home-from-home luxuries and exploring the nearby Jurassic Coast and peaceful countryside.

Being part of an estate gives head chef Dan Brown access to an abundance of ultra-fresh produce such as Red Ruby beef, rare-breed pork and chicken, and veg from the kitchen garden. His nose-to-tail cooking style aligns with Maddie and Ben's sustainability principles, so there are often home-smoked meats and less conventional cuts to try.

Modern interpretations of pub classics form a pleasingly pared-back menu. It includes dishes such as honey-roast ham hock terrine with pickled egg, Somerset cheddar and ploughman's pickle; and tomato and roasted garlic orzo risotto with elderflower plum tomatoes, crisp goat's halloumi, grilled yellow courgette and salsa verde.

Trencherman's tip

Visit for alfresco dining in summer when sourdough pizzas and small plates are served from a tin hut in the garden.

Chefs **Dan Brown** and **Danny Baker** | 3-course dinner from £42 | Seats **60** | Bedrooms **4** | Room rate from £170
cotleyinnwambrook.co.uk | Wambrook, Chard, Somerset, TA20 3EN | 01460 62348

76 The Barrington Boar

Elegant food in a characterful pub

When Alasdair Clifford returned to his home county of Somerset from London in 2018, he brought with him a host of skills honed in Michelin-starred restaurants such as Chez Bruce. They've been put to good use in the friendly environment of this contemporary country pub, which he runs with his wife Victoria Collins.

On taking over the Boar, the duo refreshed the pub's interior and menu to create a stylish setting in which to serve refined comfort food – a modest description of cooking that's nudged its way into the Estrella Damm Top 50 Gastropubs, received a mention in the *Michelin Guide* and been included in *The Good Food Guide*'s Best Local Restaurants 2024 list.

The dishes offer a taste of the local terroir and include homegrown veg from Alasdair and Victoria's market garden. Expect to feast on the likes of barbecued shoulder of lamb glazed in rose harissa with smoked aubergine and pistachio dukkah, or roast loin of sika venison with venison and bacon sausage roll, venison fat mash, damson ketchup and a red wine and peppercorn sauce.

The pud line-up features such delights as chilled vanilla rice pudding with poached Yorkshire rhubarb, gingerbread crumb and hibiscus sauce.

As well as working closely with local farmers, foragers and cheesemongers, the couple collaborate with regional breweries to stock an ever-evolving collection of drinks.

Trencherman's tip

Check out the team's new opening next door: The Barrington Bakery at Two Bakers Farm. Further dine-and-stay opportunities have also opened up with the addition of holiday lets.

Chef **Alasdair Clifford** | 3-course dinner from **£42** | Seats **45** | Bedrooms **8 plus 2 holiday homes** | Room rate from **£140**
thebarringtonboar.co.uk | Main Street, Barrington, Ilminster, Somerset, TA19 0JB | **01460 259281**

77 Holm

Rural cool in South Petherton

Making a connection to the land and local people is the driving force behind this Trencherman's Award-winning contemporary restaurant in a former bank building.

The surrounding fields supply many of the ingredients that contribute to owner Nicholas Balfe's ever-evolving menus. Formerly of esteemed London restaurants Salon, Levan and Larry's, Nicholas is careful to partner with farmers, growers, butchers, gamekeepers and fishermen who share his respect for quality ingredients.

The open-plan dining room, accented by mid-century modern furniture and artwork, provides a casual setting for the smart food. Sample it via four- and six-course tasting menus in the evenings and a set lunch during the day.

The focus of each dish is the beauty of its ingredients, as in the line-caught Dorset sea bass, which shines with the simple yet aromatic pairings of courgette, basil and elderflower.

A select and sensibly priced wine list showcases low-intervention, biodynamic and organic wines from small-scale producers.

Trencherman's tip

Nicholas and team host a bonza line-up of events year-round. Hit the terrace and its outdoor kitchen in summer for fireside suppers, DJs and bands. In the cooler months, book in for wine tastings, supper clubs and guest chef nights. Lucky overnight guests can get involved with foraging, beach trips, hill walks, meditation, mindfulness, movement and more.

Chef **Nicholas Balfe** | 4-course dinner from **£49** | Seats **30 inside, 30 outside** | Bedrooms **7**
Room rate from **£179** | **EV charging**
holmsomerset.co.uk | 28 St James's Street, South Petherton, Somerset, TA13 5BW | **01460 712470**

78 The Clockspire Restaurant and Bar

Opulent elegance in Sherborne

A visit to The Clockspire is like stepping into a bygone era, thanks to its 19th-century school-building setting of vaulted oak-beamed ceilings, polished stone floors and candelabras that hang from the rafters.

In the kitchen, head chef Luke Bryant serves up elegant modern British dishes that befit this opulent setting.

A visit to the two-AA-rosette restaurant will reveal culinary delights that increasingly use produce from the restaurant's kitchen garden. One such example is the mushroom raviolo with English asparagus, sourdough croutons and wild garlic sauce. Piscatorial pleasures come via dishes such as cured Cornish cod with New Forest strawberries, basil, elderflower dressing, radish and squid ink tuile, and dressed Cornish white crab with sea buckthorn gel, brown-crab tuile, carrot and cantaloupe melon.

Special occasion? Gather a group and opt for the A Taste of the Clockspire menu for an evening of exceptional wining and dining.

Start the evening with an aperitif at the sleek marble-topped bar on the mezzanine over the restaurant. It's a smart setting for a pre-dinner tipple from a list recognised with an AA Notable Wine List Award.

Trencherman's tip

On the last Thursday of each month, The Clockspire hosts jazz sessions for a side of bebop with dinner.

L–R: Rob Finnamore of Navas, Severino Fascendini (formerly of The Clockspire), David Hill of The Clockspire, Alex Wise of Navas

Chef **Luke Bryant** | 3-course dinner from £29 | Seats 60

theclockspire.com | Gainsborough, Milborne Port, Sherborne, Dorset, DT9 5BA | **01963 251458**

Properly crafted 0.5% IPA

staustellbrewery.co.uk

PROPER
JOB
0.5% IPA

79 Horrell & Horrell

Unique micro-dining experience

An evening spent at Horrell & Horrell is like rocking up at a foodie friend's house with a bottle of wine and letting them cook something from their garden especially for you.

Except the evening caters for 50 and takes place in a converted cow barn – in the rural village of Sparkford – on a banquet table decked out with dried fruits and flowers from the orchard and cutting patch.

Founders Jules and Steve Horrell spent 25 years working in the hospitality industry and ran two restaurants in Somerset before they launched this venture in 2023.

The novel dining experience is liberated from the formal à la carte offering. Rather than release menus, guests are treated to a surprise array of dishes championing the homegrown harvest and bounty of ingredients sourced from like-minded producers who grow, make and cure in an enviro-friendly way.

Guests tussle forks over the likes of whipped labneh, smacked cucumbers, peanut chilli crisp and borage, and chargrilled flatbreads with squash blossoms and wildflower honey.

Meals end on a sweet high with puds like Horrell & Horrell pavlova, consisting of meringue, meadowsweet cream, fig leaf custard, candied nuts, white chocolate shards and garden berries.

Additional highlights include the garden spritz on arrival (all other drinks are BYOB with no corkage fee) and the bucolic setting in which communal feasts take place.

Trencherman's tip

Check out the series of Live Fire Experience days at Horrell & Horrell's Field Kitchen.

Chef **Steve Horrell** | 3-course dinner from **£65** | Seats **50**
horrellandhorrell.co.uk | Brooklands Barn, Brains Lane, Sparkford, Somerset, BA22 7LA | **07920 816615**

80 Osip

A celebration of food, drink and design

In the artsy market town of Bruton, Osip has been making waves since it launched in 2019. Its trademark dishes are served within an ultra-contemporary barn, where an enormous window connects diners directly to the land.

Devon-born chef Merlin Labron-Johnson is known for achieving a Michelin star at London's Portland within nine months of opening. When he launched Osip, he unofficially crowned Bruton as the Somerset destination of choice for fans of the (very) good life.

The restaurant was soon awarded a Michelin star, but its Green Michelin star – acknowledging sustainable credentials – is just as pertinent, since the chef is obsessed with the integrity of ingredients.

Working in collaboration with Merlin is head chef Ciaran Brennan. The pair concoct dishes that tend to be low in meat, favouring instead an approach that centres around hero vegetables prepared in thought-provoking ways. When the team do serve meat, they use only whole animals or birds – all of which are organic and prepared in-house. Guests can enjoy expertly paired drinks whether they opt for wines or non-alcoholic alternatives.

The innovative dishes change from service to service, so menus are printed on a just-in-time basis – don't expect to be able to check it out on the website before you visit.

Trencherman's tip

For full Osip immersion, stay in one of four dreamy bedrooms. The restrained but thoughtful handcrafted finishes take inspiration from the winding rivers and bucolic pastures of Somerset – and evoke a similarly restful response.

Left to right: Bex Tonks of St. Ewe, Ciaran Brennan of Osip

Chef **Merlin Labron-Johnson** | Tasting menu **£150** | Seats **34** | Bedrooms **4** | Room rate from **£240**
osiprestaurant.com | 25 Kingsettle Hill, Hardway, Bruton, Somerset, BA10 0LN | **01749 987277**

81 Queen of Cups

Modern Middle Eastern cooking in Glasto

A pub in the heart of Glastonbury isn't the first place you'd expect to find some of the best Middle Eastern food in the country, but Queen of Cups has cemented its reputation as a multi-award-winning restaurant that surprises and delights.

Leiths graduate Ayesha Kalaji relocated to the Somerset town from London (where she cooked at Bubala, The Good Egg and The Palomar) to establish her own restaurant with friend and business partner Mary-Elizabeth O'Neill.

Drawing on her Jordanian heritage and French training, Ayesha and her talented team craft unique dishes that dazzle with their bold flavours and bright colours.

Ayesha's creative cooking and delicious execution not only saw her pick up the award for Best Chef in the Trencherman's Awards 2025, but also won her a place on the BBC's *Great British Menu* following her successful TV debut in 2023 on *MasterChef: The Professionals*. She is now a regular face across the national press and has worked on a number of chef residency programmes, both at home and abroad.

The restaurant holds Michelin Bib Gourmand status. Sourcing seasonal and local ingredients is vital, and inventive dishes include the likes of beef-shin vine-leaf chou farci, kamouneh-spiced beef-heart skewer, and fermented wild garlic labneh. Desserts are equally innovative – think ruby chocolate and raspberry crémeux infused with hibiscus.

Trencherman's tip

Check out the restaurant's custom drinks offerings thanks to collabs with a gin distillery and New Bristol Brewery. The Queen of Cups IPA is a must-try.

L–R: Ayesha Kalaji of Queen of Cups with James Hearn of Hallgarten & Novum

Chef **Ayesha Kalaji** | 3-course dinner from **£36** | Seats **45**
queenofcups.co.uk | 10–12 Northload Street, Glastonbury, Somerset, BA6 9JJ | **01458 831255**

82 The Holcombe

Eco-savvy indulgence

The Holcombe is a labour of love for owners Alan and Caroline Lucas, whose kitchen garden inspires the imaginative menus they craft for one of the most environmentally conscious restaurants in the country.

The 17th-century inn is surrounded by acres of land, which are the source of fruit, veg, herbs and flowers for the uber-seasonal menus. What can't be cultivated on-site is sourced from local producers and neighbourhood estates.

Sustainability-wise, Alan and Caroline set themselves a high bar. All food waste is composted, while used cooking oil becomes biodiesel. There are also wildlife-friendly plots among the raised beds to encourage pollinators and hedgehogs.

In the kitchen, Alan is a one-man prepping, pickling and preserving machine, finding creative new ways to use the produce from his plots and polytunnel. Everything – from the sourdough bagels and cashew-nut cheese to the ice creams and signature soufflé – is made in-house.

Flavour-packed dishes on the two-AA-rosette menus include pan-fried hake with ginger crab bisque and steamed Fowey mussels, as well as pan-fried chicken with Old Winchester cheese, garden peas and beans. Vegan creations include spiced cauliflower steak with tikka masala, garden-onion bhajis and smoked peanuts. A dessert highlight is the blackberry soufflé with warm blackberry puree and vanilla-pod ice cream.

Trencherman's tip

Book one of the gorgeous rural-luxe guest rooms or dog-friendly lodges to extend the visit – they hold a prestigious AA 5 Gold Star award.

Chef **Alan Lucas** | 3-course dinner from **£45** | Seats **45** | Bedrooms **11** | Room rate from **£170**
theholcombe.com | Stratton Road, Holcombe, Somerset, BA3 5EB | **01761 232478**

83 The Beckford Bottle Shop

Bath wining and dining

This contemporary British bistro and bottle shop in Bath pairs the sensibility of a wine merchant with the flair of a Michelin Bib Gourmand kitchen.

Inside, shelves groan with over 300 bottles, while a by-the-glass list of over 30 handpicked wines awaits exploration – ideally from a spot on one of the two comfy red sofas.

The friendly team are delighted to advise on a good pairing for guests' palates or chosen dish. Plus, there's the opportunity to grab a bottle from the shelves to take home. And on No Corkage Tuesdays, diners can dive into any bottle from the shelves without the usual fee.

This is a sociable spot, and patrons are encouraged to share seasonal small plates such as the famed Bath chaps. Wild Cornish sea bass with charcuterie velouté and cornichons and rolled Iron Age pork head with apricot ketchup provide guests with further opportunities to clash forks with their dining partners.

As seasonality is key, the dishes change regularly and draw inspiration from the team's own allotment. Here, heritage vegetables, herbs and edible flowers are cultivated, while head chef James Harris supplements the menus further with foraged finds.

The Beckford Bottle Shop is a spot to linger over pudding, and the bistro's take on the classic Maxibon ice-cream sandwich is a standout choice. Pair the almond and vanilla parfait sandwich (dipped in Valrhona chocolate) with a dessert wine from the epic wine list.

Trencherman's tip

Visiting for lunch or dinner? Take advantage of the five per cent dine-in discount on bottles to take home or enjoy at sister restaurant Beckford Canteen (just down the road).

Chef **James Harris** | 3-course dinner from **£33** | Seats **60**
beckfordbottleshop.com | 5–8 Saville Row, Bath, BA1 2QP | **01225 809302**

84 Iford Manor Kitchen

Farm-to-fork dining near Bath

Situated in a picturesque hidden valley on a 1,000-acre farming estate adjacent to Grade I-listed gardens, Iford Manor Kitchen provides exceptional farm-to-fork dining in beautiful surroundings.

The restaurant is managed by the estate's owner, William Cartwright-Hignett, lending a personal touch to the friendly service. The focus is on fresh, seasonal ingredients – many reared, grown or foraged on the estate – which executive chef Matthew Briddon and team use to craft imaginative dishes using traditional techniques.

As the seasons change, so do the menus: expect estate-raised, grass-fed meat dishes such as lamb served as a wellington with wild mushroom and truffle sauce in winter or pickled berry salad, dehydrated cabbage and baked goat's curd in summer. Pickling and preserving further extend the seasons.

Matthew is also a master charcutier and fire-cooking expert, and prepares meats in a Bertha wood oven. On Sunday lunchtimes from October to March, joints of meat are cooked specifically for the table, then carved and served by a chef for added theatre (while also reducing food waste).

Although predominantly a lunchtime restaurant, the Kitchen's regular Friday supper club (with optional wine flight) is a fabulous choice for evening dining.

Trencherman's tip

Book your place at various hands-on workshops (think sourdough, fermentation and sauces) with chef Matthew.

L-R: Debbie Daniel of Harvey & Brockless, Matthew Briddon and William and Marianne Cartwright-Hignett of Iford Manor

---

Chef **Matthew Briddon** | 3-course lunch from £55 | Seats 50
ifordmanor.co.uk/fooddrink | Iford Lane, Iford, Bath, BA15 2BA | **01225 863146**

85 Olive Tree, Bath

Bath's star turn

This chic restaurant below Bath's boutique Queensberry Hotel needs little introduction: it has held a Michelin star for seven years under executive head chef Chris Cleghorn, while its accommodation has achieved four AA rosettes and a Michelin Key.

Chris' Taste of the Season menu is available whenever the restaurant is open – lunch and dinner, regardless of the day of the week. It takes the form of three set courses, with homebaked bread and additional delights to begin and conclude the meal in style.

The entire experience costs a set £100 with no tip expected, as the restaurant's owners pride themselves on charging appropriately to provide the team with consistent, professional wages.

Each plate is built around core seasonal British ingredients (all sourced as locally as possible), and guests can journey into culinary adventures such as tender Cornish lobster, cooked over Binchotan, with Wye Valley green asparagus, jalapeño and lovage. The likes of Cornish Kern raviolo with morel, fermented Cornish Meyer lemon and Mexican marigold provide further intrigue for the palate.

For dessert, Wye Valley rhubarb with Tahitian vanilla parfait, rose and pink peppercorn meringue delivers an elegant finish. Afterwards, head to the hotel's Old Q Bar for classic digestifs from a bygone era.

Trencherman's tip

The Taste of the Season menu is the cornerstone of a very special dinner, bed and breakfast package.

Chef **Chris Cleghorn** | 3-course dinner from £70 | Seats **42** | Bedrooms **29** | Room rate from **£145**
olivetreebath.co.uk | 4–7 Russell Street, Bath, BA1 2QF | 01225 447928

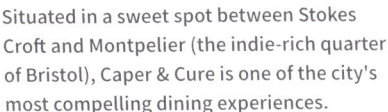

86 Caper & Cure

Neighbourhood bistro vibes in Stokes Croft

Situated in a sweet spot between Stokes Croft and Montpelier (the indie-rich quarter of Bristol), Caper & Cure is one of the city's most compelling dining experiences.

The restaurant is housed within the historic Tucketts Buildings, a department store built in the 1890s that's enjoyed many guises including a 'cash chemists', internet cafe, and arts and music venue.

However, this restaurant takeover may be the most defining moment for the building to date.

Taking a modern-European influence with a leaning toward French cuisine, the intimate restaurant is a go-to for smart and ingredient-led dishes served in a relaxed setting.

That's not to suggest this isn't the place for a special occasion. Caper & Cure offers a chef's table experience where ten gourmets feast next to the open kitchen for supper with a theatrical edge – think *The Bear* minus the intensity.

The dishes in question are crafted from the finest local and organic ingredients the crew can get their hands on, and executed in style.

A trip could involve devouring the likes of warm crab and crayfish butter with soft herbs and house bread, followed by braised Cornish octopus with cuttlefish and chorizo cassoulet.

Trencherman's tip

Chase a meal at Caper & Cure with a drop or two at sister bar Carmen Street Wine, located just behind the restaurant. The venue also hosts monthly wine tastings.

Chef **Matty Grove** | 3-course dinner from **£36** | Seats **44**
caperandcure.co.uk | 108a Stokes Croft, Bristol, BS1 3RU | **01179 232858**

87 The Queen's Arms

Elegant dining pub

Almost everything on the menu at The Queen's Arms is crafted in-house, from the nibbles at the bar through to the seasonal desserts.

Straddling the Dorset-Somerset border, the pub has a longstanding reputation for its use of homegrown ingredients. Yet, when Doune Mackenzie-Francis' family took over in 2021, they worked with head chef Rich Townsend to take the homemade ethos up a notch. Now, if something can feasibly be made in The Queen's Arms kitchen, it is – resulting in a menu of hyper-seasonal dishes.

Anything Rich and his team can't craft themselves is sourced from quality local producers. The line-up includes Montgomery Cheddar in North Cadbury, vegetables, herbs and soft fruit from Doune and other individuals in the village, meat from Blackmore Vale butchers (and pork from Doune when available), and ice cream from Ecco Gelato in Sherborne.

Sample the quality ingredients in elevated pub dishes such as garlic and rosemary marinated lamb with caponata, courgette, black olives, basil and lamb sauce, or caramelised honey tart with poached garden plums and almond gelato.

Five bedrooms above the pub are individually decorated with handpicked antiques and fabrics from the likes of Colefax and Fowler. There are also three dog-friendly rooms in the Coach House and a family-friendly cottage (also dog friendly) with two bedrooms situated in the peaceful garden behind the pub.

Stay the night to explore the many surrounding walkways. Ramblers and cyclists can enjoy great food on the go via the pub's excellent takeaway menu.

Trencherman's tip

Guests should keep an eye out for Doune's cookery classes, which take place in her own kitchen.

Chef **Rich Townsend** | 3-course dinner from **£45** | Seats **60** | Bedrooms **10** | Room rate from **£140** | **EV charging**
thequeensarms.com | Corton Denham, Sherborne, Somerset, DT9 4LR | **01963 220317**

88 Da Costa

A bite of Italy in Bruton

Somerset's raved-about town is a magnet for gourmets, and this impressive Italian eatery rooted in tradition is a key crowd-puller.

Da Costa is part of Artfarm, a collective comprising unique destinations that draw together art, nature and community. Other notable additions include fellow Bruton business Roth Bar and The Groucho Club in Soho.

The restaurant is inspired by Artfarm co-founder Iwan Wirth's maternal grandfather, who originated from a small mountainous village in the Veneto region of northern Italy. He later emigrated to Switzerland, where he opened a restaurant heralded for its simple, honest fare.

A century later (and 800 miles, give or take, from that first restaurant), Da Costa is carrying on his legacy. Yet it also marks the start of an exciting new chapter in the culinary story.

Head chef Robert Smart remains true to northern Italian recipes but gives them a Somerset spin through the use of freshly grown, seasonal ingredients from the restaurant's walled garden and surrounding area.

This fusion results in antipasti dishes such as Durslade Farm beef carpaccio with mustard, canederli with spinach and cheddar fondue, and gnocchi fritto with mortadella and fresh cheese.

Of course, homemade pastas and risottos are big hitters on the menu, as are the wood-fired specials (the Durslade Farm lamb with creamy polenta and Da Costa sauce is a firm fave).

Trencherman's tip

The tiramisu is so good it should be illegal. The classic pud is also available to share between three rule-breaking chums.

Chef **Robert Smart** | 3-course dinner from **£40** | Seats **74**
da-costa.co.uk | Durslade Farm, Dropping Lane, Bruton, Somerset, BA10 0NL | **01749 467880**

89 Homewood

Elegantly eccentric

Expect the unexpected at this luxurious spa hotel just outside Bath; nothing about the gabled Georgian mansion is quite what it seems.

Roll up to the entrance to be welcomed by Oswald, a giant monkey deep in thought. Check in amid a reception area dominated by a wall of antique clocks. And book one of the best rooms to discover artistic flourishes and a host of modern amenities – plus a private hot tub, barrel sauna and icy plunge pool.

For a more communal thermal experience, Homewood's spa offers an outdoor vitality pool, indoor and outdoor saunas, hydrotherapy pool, steam room, plus outdoor hot tub and swimming pool with views of the Avon Valley.

The playful indulgence continues in the luxurious Olio restaurant. Here, Jamie Forman's menus showcase British dishes with a Mediterranean twist, made using local and kitchen-garden-grown produce. Explore dishes such as the South West spare-rib pulled pork, whole branzino sea bass and ember-roasted beets.

Or take a table at its Med-inspired feasting space, La Taberna, a vibrant canvas orangery bedecked with chandeliers and colourful fabrics. Begin with a glass of Champagne while taking a whistlestop tour of the kitchen garden, then dive into bountiful sharing boards brimming with hand-picked veg and freshly baked breads. Follow with stuffed lamb and porchetta, cooked on the grill in front of guests and accompanied by masses of veg from the no-dig garden.

Trencherman's tip

Overnight guests can take advantage of a communal larder and variety of complimentary snacks and drinks.

Chef **Jamie Forman** | 3-course dinner from **£60** | Seats **80** | Bedrooms **31** | Room rate from **£205** | **EV charging**
homewoodbath.co.uk | Abbey Lane, Freshford, Bath, BA2 7TB | **01225 580439**

90 Yak Yeti Yak

Authentic Nepalese cuisine

When Sarah and Sera Gurung settled in the UK in 2004, they opened the nation's first purely Nepalese restaurant in the basement of one of Bath's grand Georgian townhouses.

Inspired by the couple's travels, and evenings spent in small Himalayan tea shops enjoying meals cooked by some of the world's lesser-known culinary heroes, Yak Yeti Yak was a place for them to indulge in the food they loved. The unique offering was a hit with the locals, so much so that within a couple of years they moved the restaurant to a roomier basement on Pierrepont Street.

Everything is cooked by Sarah and Sera in the Yak Yeti Yak kitchen, from the handmade steamed momos (delicately spiced traditional Nepalese dumplings) to the chutneys and marinades.

Staying true to Nepalese cuisine, around half of the dishes are vegetarian or vegan and include standouts such as aloo tamar: fermented bamboo shoots braised with black-eyed peas, new potatoes and fresh tomato, flavoured with cumin and freshly ground aromatic spices.

Dessert is no less authentic, with the likes of Kulfi-style ice cream with dark chocolate and stem ginger bringing the meal to a close with a hint of heat.

Trencherman's tip

Choose between conventional tables and chairs, floor-level tables with cushions, or alfresco dining in the courtyard.

Chefs **Sarah and Sera Gurung** | 3-course dinner from **£26** | Seats **60**
yakyetiyak.co.uk | 12 Pierrepont Street, Bath, BA1 1LA | **01225 442299**

91 Chez Dominique

Parisian charm in Bath

This family-owned restaurant has established itself as a firm favourite in well-heeled Bath. It occupies a prime spot close to Pulteney Bridge, one of the most photographed examples of Georgian architecture in the city, and has a private dining room overlooking the weir.

Husband-and-wife owners Chris Tabbitt and Sarah Olivier opened the doors in 2016, naming the restaurant after their first child Dominic.

Today, it radiates French bistro charm, reflecting Chris's experience in classical French and British cuisines at establishments including Bibendum in London's Michelin House.

Head chef Sam Lewis uses the freshest South West ingredients to create a seasonal menu bursting with flavours. He showcases multiple techniques, as evidenced in dishes such as scallops with merguez sausage and fregola ragu and smoked tomato sauce, or Creedy

Carver duck breast with pak choi, sweet potato puree and crisps together with a ginger, honey and five-spice sauce. Keep it français for dessert with the griottine cherry clafoutis with vanilla ice cream.

The wine list has been revamped and includes plenty of new and exciting bottles, with French classics sitting alongside stunning finds from further afield. Warm and attentive service completes this pleasingly Parisian experience in the heart of Bath.

Trencherman's tip

Visit at lunchtime (or Sunday to Thursday between 5 and 6pm at certain times of the year), for the set-price menu. Four-legged friends are welcome at lunchtime too.

Chef **Sam Lewis** | 3-course dinner from **£34** | Seats **40**
chezdominique.co.uk | 15 Argyle Street, Bathwick, Bath, BA2 4BQ | **01225 463482**

Emberwood

Welcoming city dining

Georgian-inspired interiors with a gleaming modern twist await at this restaurant within the Francis Hotel. Opened in May 2025, as part of a multimillion-pound restoration of one of Bath's most iconic addresses, Emberwood's plush velvets, lush plants, soft banquettes and marble tables are the epitome of glamour.

Sparkling chandeliers, subtle lighting, pillars and considered decor create an atmosphere that's further elevated by an open kitchen which allows diners to watch the chefs flame-cook dishes.

At the twinkling bar, guests socialise while sipping curated cocktails designed by Zoe Burgess from Atelier Pip. A Wonky Manhattan, for example, involves adding a splash of Somerset Pomona to Redwood Empire Rye, vermouth and bitters.

In the kitchen, executive head chef David Hazell exhibits his passion for cooking over fire to achieve deep flavours. Creedy Carver chicken from Devon, dayboat Cornish hake and sun-ripened Isle of Wight tomatoes are just a few of the quality local ingredients given due respect over charcoal.

Start with crispy Porthilly oysters or coal-roasted scallops dripping in garlic butter. Follow with dry-aged côte de boeuf and beef-fat béarnaise or whole monkfish tail wrapped in lardo.

For a sweet finish, the signature rhubarb and custard with white chocolate is a must (although a glossy yuzu-curd choux bun from the retro-glam dessert trolley is not to be overlooked).

Trencherman's tip

In summer, plush cushions on the terrace invite guests to settle in for lunch alfresco while marvelling at the historic handsomeness of Bath's iconic Queen Square.

Chef **David Hazell** | 3-course dinner from **£80** | Seats **100** | Bedrooms **98** | Room rate from **£200** | **EV charging**
emberwoodbath.com | No.5 Queen Square, Bath, BA1 2HH | **01225 473351**

93 Corkage

Convivial dining

Corkage embodies the rustic charm of a continental neighbourhood bistro, exuding the kind of cosy intimacy that sees the team on first-name terms with guests.

Originally a pop-up venture conceived by pals Richard Knighting and Marty Grant, this is now one of Bath's most loved and award-winning dining destinations.

The premise is simple: a rotation of seasonal plates is paired with a handpicked curation of wines, available by the glass or bottle. If you're bowled over by a particular drop, pick up a bottle to take home.

When the pair opened Corkage, their aim was to create a place that would encourage conviviality and conversation. Sharing is actively encouraged, so don't be shy about ordering multiple plates from the creative line-up and digging in with your nearest and dearest.

Conveniently split into veggie, fish and meat dishes, the ever-evolving menu features the likes of marinated Isle of Wight tomatoes with basil sorbet and wild garlic dressing, pan-roasted cod fillet with braised cannellini beans, chorizo and onion soubise, and the overnight-roast pork belly served with satay sauce, fennel and broccolini.

Chef Rob Thompson's high-calibre cooking is taken to giddy heights by Richard and Marty's passion for wine. The duo's instinct for pairing is exceptional, so take the opportunity to sample something new.

Trencherman's tip

Take a seat in the newly refurbished Georgian courtyard garden. It's a serene haven and an idyllic spot for alfresco dining and relaxed convos.

Chef **Rob Thompson** | 3-course dinner from **£35** | Seats **55**
corkagebath.com | 5 Chapel Row, Bath, BA1 1HN | **01225 423417**

94 Robun

Modern take on Japanese yakiniku

This smart restaurant in the centre of Bath offers a refreshing alternative to the city's many brasseries and brunch spots. Crafting a modern take on Japanese yakiniku (the art of grilling meat, seafood and vegetables over a traditional robata charcoal fire), sushi and sashimi, Robun has established itself as one of the region's most exciting dining spots – evidenced by its Michelin Plate status.

Cult Japanese classics like tempura and gyoza plus bao buns feature on the menus, but be sure to browse more creative dishes. These include chef's selection of fresh, sliced sushi and nigiri, black cod, soft shell crab futomaki with kimchi mayo and wow-factor wagyu beef tataki served with truffle teriyaki and pepper sauce.

For a culinary journey across Japan, opt for the Taste of Robun. The eight-course menu is best paired with the house sake (the sake menu is one of the most extensive in the region) and wine recommendations.

Special attention is paid to matching the temperature of the sake to each dish, so the meal begins with a cool sake paired with citrus edamame and progresses to a warmer sake to complement the flavour of black cod.

Aga, Robun's GM, has a background in fine dining and a love of innovative hospitality. This experience and passion combined create an atmosphere that's both buzzy and welcoming.

Trencherman's tip

Explore the intriguing sake, Japanese whisky and cocktail list. The talented bar team have curated a bespoke line-up of cocktails which includes the likes of smoked mezcal Negronis and a sake-infused Tom Collins.

Chef **Kasae Fraser** | 3-course dinner from **£29** | Seats **76**
robun.co.uk | 4 Princes Buildings, George Street, Bath, BA1 2ED | **01225 433200**

True egg perfection

steweeggs.com

St.Ewe
Delicious Free Range Eggs

95 Chequers

Gastropub in Bath's poshest postcode

Church pew banquettes, deep grey walls and parquet flooring with light flooding in from large Georgian sash windows: Chequers certainly cuts a dash as a smart traditional pub.

Set in a townhouse on an elegant street in Bath's famously dapper neighbourhood (the Circus and the Royal Crescent are just around the corner), Chequers offers something for everyone – from casual cocktails and cosy lunches to the full dinner experience.

The kitchen team, led by head chef Sam Stone, work with independent suppliers, including ethical and sustainable farmers. All fish specials are sourced directly from South West dayboats to ensure the very best produce graces the plates.

Go the whole hog with a starter of Cornish octopus with 'nduja, anchovy gremolata, aioli and kale, followed by West End Farm pork collar with celeriac remoulade, black pudding, pea, gooseberry and cider jus, or opt for the Cornish mackerel with clams, Jersey Royals, baby leeks, sea lettuce and pickled apple.

Pair your pick of the food with a traditional ale, chic cocktail or vibrant wine.

Trencherman's tip

This is a favourite haunt for locals, so don't leave without striking up a conversation to get the full Chequers community experience.

Chef **Sam Stone** | 3-course dinner from **£45** | Seats **80**
chequersbath.net | 50 Rivers Street, Bath, BA1 2QA | **01225 428924**

96 BANK

Flaming hearty food

Set in a former Lloyds Bank building less than a ten-minute walk from Bristol Temple Meads Station, neighbourhood restaurant BANK enjoys a city-wide reputation for its contemporary flame-cooked food.

Crisp white walls, offset by navy wood panelling and caramel-leather banquettes, sit beneath exposed lightbulbs in an easy-going atmosphere. At BANK, fire is treated more like seasoning than a method of cooking and is incorporated into every dish on the menu – even desserts.

Head chef and co-owner Jack Briggs-Horan is a true champion of local ingredients. All meat is sourced from within a 30-mile radius, while vegetables are harvested from the restaurant's own smallholding.

While BANK enjoys a loyal following for its Sunday lunch (voted among the top 50 in the country by *The Good Food Guide*), the main menu features a generous selection of innovative dishes, the ingredients of which change regularly to reflect the seasons and Jack's penchant for fusing flavours from different cultures.

Landrace pork chop is pimped with miso mustard sauce and grilled shallot, beef shin nugget is doused in Dorset Red custard and jalapeño butter, and jerk wild duck shares plate space with sweet potato and a hot rhubarb sauce.

Special occasion? Plump for one of the larger sharing mains, perfect as a showstopping centrepiece when feasting with friends.

Trencherman's tip

Check out Lapin, BANK's new French bistro-style sister restaurant on Bristol Harbour, where 60 wines are available by the glass.

Chef **Jack Briggs-Horan** | 3-course dinner from **£29** | Seats **42**
bankbristol.com | 107 Wells Road, Totterdown, Bristol, BS4 2BS | **0117 4527536**

97 Harbour House

Waterside dining in Bristol

On balmy summer evenings in Bristol, few restaurants can compete with Harbour House's waterside location for post-work drinks and supper against a backdrop of paddleboarders and kayakers.

The Harbour House building makes for an unusual and pleasing dining setting; it's said to have been designed by Isambard Kingdom Brunel as his private boathouse. It was also the site of Banksy's first solo exhibition in 2000.

In its current incarnation, it's a pleasingly rustic restaurant with vaulted ceilings and verdant plants, all of which create a relaxed and airy vibe. Outside, the balcony experience has been elevated by the addition of an awning.

The informality extends to the food offering, which is seasonal and sustainable, majoring on all-day dining and freshly caught seafood. The kitchen has upped the ante recently and is working with a feast of delicious suppliers.

Gorge on dishes like cured monkfish with pickled ginger and greek yogurt, or roast cod with saffron-infused lobster bisque and wild garlic stems. Or try the surf and turf: a 12oz bone-in sirloin with glazed king prawns, seasonal greens and king oyster mushrooms.

The delectable dishes are bolstered by an equally impressive drinks list. A broad selection of beers shares cellar space with an expansive selection of English sparkling wines – to such an extent that there's no longer Champagne on the menu.

Trencherman's tip

Swing by during the early evening to enjoy the harbour's chilled vibe via carefully crafted cocktails at a table on deck.

Chef **Altin Ndoja** | 3-course dinner from **£30** | Seats **100**
hhbristol.com | The Grove, Bristol, BS1 4RB | **0117 9251212**

98 Lapin

Gloriously Gallic

French in flavour and heart, yet resolutely Bristolian in attitude, Lapin is the latest opening from the team behind BANK in Totterdown.

Housed on Wapping Wharf, part of Bristol's historic floating harbour, the compact bistro is building a notable reputation for its casual and contemporary take on classic French cooking and Gallic vibes. Its other claim to fame is a fabulous wine list of over 60 French bottles available by the glass, which may well be the best of its type in the region.

Inside, Lapin nails the laid-back bistro aesthetic: chalkboard menus, sage green walls, wooden tables and wine bottles lining the shelves.

A daily prix fixe menu offers good value for a casual lunch, but the full à la carte encourages indulgence. Discover dishes such as confit duck leg with spring cassoulet and kielbasa, pork schnitzel with peas, bacon and morels, and roast duck crown à l'orange – served to share – with bigarade sauce and braised chicory.

Chef-owner Jack Briggs-Horan (also exec chef at BANK) draws inspiration from his childhood holidays in France and crafts his seasonally inspired menus using ingredients from trusted local growers, farmers, butchers and fishmongers. Produce from the team's own allotment on the outskirts of Bath also appears regularly.

Trencherman's tip

The epic wine list is grouped by style to encourage guests to broaden their horizons. Unsure where to start? Ask for restaurant manager Carole Petitbois, the palate behind the wine selection.

Chef **Jack Briggs-Horan** | 3-course dinner from **£29** | Seats **44**
lapinbristol.co.uk | Unit 14, Cargo 2, Museum Street, Bristol, BS1 6ZA | **01174 084997**

99 Noah's

Sumptuous seafood suppers

This fish-and-chip restaurant may blow others out of the water when it comes to the signature dish, but it's when diving into the full seafood line-up that diners discover a veritable feast of piscatorial pleasures.

Wife-and-husband team Joie and Dan Rosser are the duo behind relaxed riverside restaurant Noah's (named after their son), tucked under the flyover at Cumberland Basin.

They've created a dining experience that majors on the culture-defining dish of battered fish and thick-cut chips (with homemade mushy peas, a slice of lemon and tartare sauce, naturally) but with serious provenance creds. There are just 24 hours between the line-caught haddock landing at Newlyn market to Dan coating it in a light beer batter ready for frying.

Seafood from regional coastal markets, as well as shores across Scotland, inspires the rest of the enticing catch-to-kitchen menu.

While the menu changes daily, an array of shellfish and grilled fish dishes with complementary dressings always feature.

Delve in with hand-dived, grilled Orkney scallops, served in the shell with a cloak of garlic butter and fresh herbs. Then, if not committed to the signature serve, feast on seared ray wing served with romesco or brown butter and a choice of potatoes, chips or seasonal veg.

Everyone is made to feel welcome by the team thanks to a range of inclusive dietary menus (vegan dishes available on request) and choices for little ones.

Trencherman's tip

Dan and Joie strive to make Noah's as affordable as possible, an effort reflected in the Kids Eat Free school-holiday special and the keenly priced Lock Keeper's Menu (available every lunchtime and from 5–6.30pm Monday to Thursday).

Chef **Dan Rosser** | 3-course dinner from **£32.95** | Seats **54 inside, 30 outside**
www.noahsbristol.co.uk | 1 Brunel Lock Road, Bristol, BS1 6XS | **01174 529240**

100 Escala Tapas

A taste of Spain in Somerset

You don't need to hit the city for quality tapas when Escala, in the coastal setting of Clevedon's beach and pier, delivers an authentic experience by the bucketload.

The one-AA-rosette restaurant offers laid-back small plates from a kitchen headed up by chef Josh Orman.

The menu is switched up multiple times each week, reflecting the team's ethos of crafting dishes that are ultra seasonal. Quality is paramount, as revealed in the provenance of the top-notch produce surfing its way onto the menu. Expect speciality ingredients imported from Spain (including a whopping selection of wines) and fish that's been freshly landed on South West shores.

Start with the satisfying crunch and smooth interior of sweet potato, red pepper and goat's cheese croquettes. In this setting, it would be criminal not to move on to seafood plates, so try the pescado: whole-baked megrim sole with grilled lemon and mojo verde. Or there's the equally lip-smacking gambas pil pil of whole Atlantic prawns in chilli and garlic.

Meat dishes are just as memorable, with the likes of smoke-cured pork belly and pickled green chilli showcasing the kitchen's flair for fermentation and flavour.

Owners Dom and Alex Lamy also own Vintage & Vine just a few minutes away. The bottle shop, bar and small plates venue is a cracking spot for a pre-dinner tipple.

Trencherman's tip

It's impossible to ignore the attractive bottles, tins and jars of speciality ingredients lining the shelves. Purchase them at the restaurant to recreate the authentic Spanish experience at home.

Chef **Josh Orman** | Dishes from **£6–£16** | Seats **52**
escalatapas.co.uk | 12 The Beach, Clevedon, Somerset, BS21 7QU | **01275 217600**

Wiltshire & Gloucestershire

Wiltshire & Gloucestershire

Numbers on the map correspond to the numbers next to the restaurants in the guide.

TEWKESBURY

106
Shurdington

CHELTENHAM

GLOUCESTER

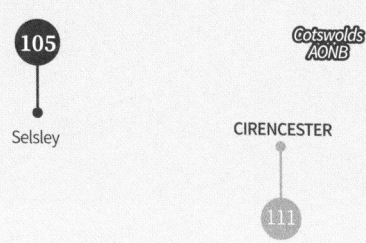
Cotswolds
AONB

105
Selsley

CIRENCESTER

111

MALMESBURY

103
104
Castle Combe

110

SWINDON

Lacock

102

109

BRADFORD-ON-AVON

Edington

108

101
Horningsham

WARMINSTER

107

101 The Bath Arms at Longleat

Countryside dining from The Beckford Group

Named one of the 100 best places to stay in the UK by _The Times_, The Bath Arms is a traditional yet stylish country inn on the edge of the Longleat Estate in Wiltshire.

The relaxed, dog-friendly venue, just two hours from London and 30 minutes from Bath, is a charming environment in which to linger over a long lunch or sumptuous supper.

Chef Jack Chapman and his talented team are committed to utilising the abundant seasonal Wiltshire produce on their doorstep, including the fruits of their herb garden. Meat and game are sourced from local farms and the Longleat Estate itself, while the fish is landed daily on the south coast.

The menu is carefully designed to reflect each season. Sample red mullet with Brixham crab and Yorkshire rhubarb, try skrei cod with chicken-fat leek, parsley crumb, chicken butter sauce and crispy leeks, or go all out

with the Dartmoor venison striploin with celeriac dauphinoise, poached blackberries and anise jus.

The bar is stocked with traditional ales (many locally brewed, including the inn's own Horning Ale) and world-class wines from sister venue The Beckford Bottle Shop in Bath. The spirits collection has become increasingly local and includes the pub's own brand of gin, produced in nearby Frome.

Delicious snacks are available throughout the day. In summer, dining spills out onto the sunny terrace and into the lush gardens. Here, live music, barbecues and fire-cooked dining events are highlights of the season.

Trencherman's tip

Book one of the 16 bedrooms for a chic dine and stay experience.

Chef **Jack Chapman** | 3-course dinner from **£40** | Seats **74** | Bedrooms **16** | Room rate from **£100**
batharmsinn.com | Horningsham, Warminster, Wiltshire, BA12 7LY | **01985 844308**

102 The Bunch of Grapes

New-wave cooking at an ancient pub

A family-run pub in a rural town may be an unlikely setting for new-wave gastronomy, but it's where chef Tony Casey plays with flavour, texture and style to create dishes that dazzle.

Run by husband and wife team Tony Casey and Maylee Speller, The Bunch of Grapes holds a Michelin recommendation, an entry in *The Good Food Guide* and two AA rosettes. It also won Muddy Stilettos' Best Restaurant in Wiltshire 2025.

Kickstart your visit with cocktails while you ponder whether to plump for à la carte or push the boat out with the seven-course tasting menu. Either way, quality seasonal ingredients take centre stage in dishes like Isle of Wight tomatoes with chervil juice, balsamic jelly, fermented radish and pine nuts. Or indulge in the rich flavours of local duck breast with plum,

butternut squash terrine, pak choi and confit leg spring roll.

For those seeking something more casual, the bar menu offers pub classics as well as snacks like salt and pepper squid with garlic mayo and cheese and truffle arancini.

The interior styling is easy on the eye. An imposing bar with an impressive collection of spirits and glassware provides the focal point while, on the first floor, striking blue walls and eye-catching artwork deliver a visual feast to complement the cooking.

Trencherman's tip

Sister business Fig, which comprises a deli, bakery and shop, has recently opened in The Shambles. Visit for epic brunches and bakes.

Chefs **Tony Casey and Łukasz Mielnik** | 3-course dinner from **£32.50** | Seats **60**
thebunchofgrapes.com | 14 Silver Street, Bradford-on-Avon, Wiltshire, BA15 1JY | **01225 863650**

103 The Manor House

Exquisite elegance in the countryside

In the picturesque Cotswolds village of Castle Combe, The Manor House exudes a magnetic energy that begins on the winding drive that leads to the 14th-century retreat.

There's a dining experience for every occasion, with a Michelin-starred restaurant, alfresco options, the Time Bar with over 100 gins, lounges for coffee and afternoon tea, and private dining rooms. The team also run a pub in the village (The Castle Inn).

Taking its name from the river that runs through the hotel grounds, the Bybrook restaurant is the jewel in The Manor House's crown. Executive chef Rob Potter has retained a Michelin star here since 2017. He and his brigade create exceptional seasonal dishes from local and British ingredients, enhanced by expertly matched fine wines.

The team have introduced a four-course menu in addition to the knockout full tasting experience. Feast on mains such as dover sole with wild herbs, N25 oscietra caviar and Irish seaweed butter, and Huntsham Farm middle white pork with celeriac, turnip, chard and black garlic. While every dish is exquisitely elegant, the dessert of alphonso mango with coconut, passionfruit and kaffir lime is standout.

Diners who stay over in the manor house or its mews cottages can spend time exploring 365 acres of grounds, including Italian gardens and an 18-hole championship golf course, plus Castle Combe village and many Cotswold walks.

Trencherman's tip

Romantic getaway? Explore the Bybrook Dine & Stay package: signature tasting menu for two, a room of your choice and an excellent breakfast.

Chef **Robert Potter** | Signature tasting menu **£145** | Seats **75** | Bedrooms **50** | Room rate from **£295** | **EV charging**
exclusive.co.uk/the-manor-house | Castle Combe, Chippenham, Wiltshire, SN14 7HX | 01249 782206

104 The Castle Inn

Exceptional experience with local charm

The Cotswolds village of Castle Combe, with its honey-coloured cottages and picture-postcard setting, has often been hailed as the prettiest village in England, but its most delightful asset is undoubtedly The Castle Inn.

The 12th-century pub with rooms treats diners to a thoughtfully curated menu of seasonally inspired dishes. It was crowned Best Trencherman's Pub in 2023 and has picked up a Michelin listing.

Since then, James Boniface has taken up the head chef mantle. Through his own philosophy of *keep it local, make it accessible*, his graceful but generous menu continues the pub's already-cemented reputation for beautiful flavour combinations.

Such skilful cooking is effortlessly demonstrated in James' new menu. It features knockout plates such as beef short rib with beef-dripping

waffle, duck liver parfait, cavolo nero and sweet potato puree, as well as hake with pink fir potato, silverskin onions, clams, chilli garlic and lemon butter.

Sweet-toothed diners will find it impossible to avoid a helping of sticky toffee pudding with prune and ginger puree, vanilla ice cream and candied walnuts to finish.

Drinks are sourced with as much care as the food, and the list includes fellow B-Corp business Toast. This brewery crafts ale from surplus bread to reduce food waste and donates all its profits to a charity with the same aim.

Trencherman's tip

Make a night of it and stay in one of 12 immaculately furnished rooms.

Chef **James Boniface** | 3-course dinner from **£41** | Seats **40** | Bedrooms **12** | Room rate from **£160** | **EV charging**
thecastleinn.co.uk | West Street, Castle Combe, Chippenham, Wiltshire, SN14 7HN | **01249 783030**

105 The Bell Inn

Greedily good Cotswold pub

Traditional country pubs may be ten a penny in the Cotswolds, but it's rare to find one that's a proper dog-friendly local which also crafts award-winning gourmet dishes.

At The Bell Inn, visitors are just as welcome to turn up in wellies for a pint and a pickled egg with a four-legged friend in tow as they are when dressed to indulge in a smart three-course feast.

Chef-proprietor Mark Payne has recently welcomed Martyn Davies to the kitchen as head chef. The new appointment signals a continuation of the inn's long-held ethos: crafting standout dishes from hyperlocal, seasonal produce. Lamb comes from a neighbouring field, while vegetables are picked straight from Mark's own allotment and kitchen garden.

The menu is refreshingly simple and places emphasis on quality ingredients cooked well. Dining options range from a lunchtime menu of pub classics, smaller bites and sandwiches on homemade sourdough, to dinner dishes that include the likes of whipped homemade basil ricotta with Wye Valley asparagus and marinated courgette salad. In winter, a rich slow-cooked blade of Gloucestershire beef with fondant potato, pea puree and king oyster mushroom is a house staple – and a must-order.

For pudding, indulge in the likes of dark-chocolate olive oil cake with white chocolate ice cream and pistachio oil.

Trencherman's tip

The inn stocks 50 artisan gins – many distilled locally. Book a room for the night to let loose and explore the intriguing list.

Chefs **Mark Payne and Martyn Davies** | 3-course dinner from **£32** | Seats **58** | Bedrooms **3** | Room rate from **£90**

thebellinnselsley.com | Bell Lane, Selsley, Gloucestershire, GL5 5JY | **01453 753801**

106 The Greenway Hotel and Spa

Historic hideaway

Eight acres of lush countryside on the outskirts of Cheltenham form the backdrop to this 16th-century Elizabethan manor, where lavish Elan Spa treatments are complemented by intricate dining in a tranquil setting.

The Greenway has been a luxury hotel since it was bought out of private ownership in 1946. In 2011, the polished Cotswolds getaway (which takes its name from the pre-Roman path running alongside its grounds) became part of the prestigious Eden Hotel Collection – which won the AA Small Hotel Group of the Year 2024/2025.

The hotel's three-AA-rosette The Garden Room Restaurant has, fittingly, views of a sunken garden and ornate lily pond. And it's here, on crisp white tablecloths, that top-tier dinners, Sunday lunches and luxurious afternoon teas provide equal levels of indulgence.

Chef Abhijit Dasalkar puts his creative spin on modern British classics in an à la carte menu that shifts with the seasons. Dishes like Brixham plaice stuffed with scallop mousse rubs shoulders with fusion creations such as char siu pork, Orkney scallop dim sum, and ponzu sauce with chilli and garlic oil.

Desserts further demonstrate the restaurant's ethos of building dishes around seasonal and local ingredients, for example the summer dish of lemon delice with herb sorbet and raspberry consommé. There's also an excellent selection of British cheeses.

Trencherman's tip

For a casual lunch, head to the hotel's Orchard Brasserie and feast on bento boxes inspired by Mexican, Mediterranean and Japanese flavours.

Chef **Abhijit Dasalkar** | 3-course dinner from **£67.50** | Seats **24** | Bedrooms **21** | Room rate from **£209**
thegreenwayhotelandspa.com | Shurdington, Cheltenham, Gloucestershire, GL51 4UG | **01242 862352**

107 Bishopstrow Hotel & Spa

Playful country pile

This country hotel offers a playful and refreshing reinvention of the manor house experience. Georgian elegance is balanced with modern-day sass in bedrooms packed with delicious colours, quirky features and lush views.

The jumping-off point for any visit here, however, is a meal at The Garden Grill, a farm-to-fork restaurant with a no-dig garden at its heart. Seasonal fruit, veg and herbs are grown using organic and sustainable methods, providing flavour and freshness all year round.

The restaurant is headed up by Philip Lewis, a man with swanky creds: he has previously cheffed at British hotel institutions The Balmoral in Edinburgh and Brown's Hotel in Mayfair

While the menu is invitingly relaxed (several dishes can be ordered as starters or mains), there is ample opportunity to worship at the tasty altar of old-school posh grub, too.

That said, this is also a fantastic spot for enjoying simple but beautifully prepared dishes such as South West scallops, ultra-fresh chicory, fig and pear salad, or a pillowy comforting classic in the form of Godminster cheese soufflé.

Notwithstanding the fine food, Bishopstrow attains bougie Wiltshire getaway status with its boutique spa. Unwind with a soothing treatment, then get hot and unbothered in the steam and sauna room before sliding down to the restaurant, relaxed to the max.

Trencherman's tip

This spot is worth a stopover. Stay the night in a room with a private outdoor jacuzzi, explore the 18th-century temple and walled garden, and take a riverside stroll in a pair of Le Chameau boots from the welly wall.

Chef **Philip Lewis** | 3-course dinner from £40 | Seats **60** | Bedrooms **36** | Room rate from £**220** | **EV charging**
bishopstrowhotel.com | Boreham Road, Warminster, Wiltshire, BA12 9HH | **01985 804680**

108 The Three Daggers

Multifaceted dining

Comprising a dining pub with rooms, farm shop, microbrewery and cottages, The Three Daggers offers a food-focused retreat in a bucolic countryside setting.

The dining pub centres on hyper-local cooking, with exec chef Toby Sharpe shaping the menus around the ripe and slow-grown produce from the pub's own farm.

The kitchen crew crafts these fresh ingredients into elevated dishes like cured prosciutto with charred peach, soused peach puree, croutons, leaves, buttermilk and pickled mustard seeds.

Toby and team ensure the menu doesn't stray into pub predictability. Other flavour-packed creations include dayboat fish with spiced red lentil dhal, mint chutney, bhaji onions, and greens.

Those who can't resist the lure of a pub burger find satiation in stacked compilations like korean fried chicken slathered in American-style cheese and a hot honey glaze, served with kimchi slaw and spiced fries.

In summer, Toby ignites the wood-fired oven to cook up bubbling pizzas piled with seasonal, home-grown toppings.

All of the field-to-fork dishes are best paired with a small-batch beer from the microbrewery.

Trencherman's tip

Holidaying in one of the charming rustic cottages? First things first: visit The Three Daggers' farm shop with an empty XL tote. It's imperative to stuff it with quality produce from the farm, plus local artisan goodies, for impeccable snacking throughout your stay.

Chef **Toby Sharpe** | 3-course dinner from **£30** | Seats **80** | Bedrooms **16** | Room rate from **£95**
threedaggers.co.uk | 47 Westbury Road, Edington, Westbury, Wiltshire, BA13 4PG | **01380 830940**

109 Sign of the Angel

Romantic inn steeped in history

Visitors flock to the National Trust village of Lacock for its cobbled streets and stone cottages. They've graced the screens of many a costume drama, including *Downton Abbey* and *Pride and Prejudice*.

In-the-know gastronomes make a beeline for Sign of the Angel (Lacock's only two-AA-rosette restaurant), a 15th-century coaching inn that oozes olde-worlde charm while crafting modern British food.

Sustainable, local produce forms the bedrock of dishes such as venison haunch with beetroot, rainbow chard, king oyster mushrooms, celeriac and horseradish puree and peppercorn sauce. Showstopper desserts include the likes of dark chocolate and brandy delice with honeycomb, strawberries and cream.

Well-executed classics are not in short supply either and take the form of dishes such as battered Cornish fish and triple-cooked chips, and burgers with chorizo jam (a mushroom

and pine nut alternative is available for vegetarians). Plus, there's always a comforting pie of the day to be had.

Stop by during the daytime to take advantage of the three tapas-style dishes served with olives and bread, or make a night of it and book one of the five homely rooms. Each has original period features, which make for a quintessentially English country-inn experience.

Trencherman's tip

The relaxing pub is a charmingly romantic spot at any time of the year. In summer, while away the hours in the suntrap garden devouring small plates or a cream tea. Winter provides the opportunity to cosy up by the wood burners and dine by candlelight.

Chef **Jamie Barnett** | 3-course dinner from **£40** | Seats **50** | Bedrooms **5** | Room rate from **£120**

signoftheangel.co.uk | 6 Church Street, Lacock, Chippenham, Wiltshire, SN15 2LB | **01249 730230**

110 The Old Bell Hotel

Culinary magic in an ancient setting

If peak dining is a finely tuned alchemy of cuisine, service and ambience, it's achieved to great effect here in the shade of an ancient abbey in the market town of Malmesbury. But what takes the Cotswolds address next level is something more enigmatic. It's the thrill of time travel.

As if Kim and Whit Hanks weren't spellbound enough when they first took the reins of the Grade I-listed, 800-year-old hotel (rumoured to be England's oldest), discovering their ancestors owned it many centuries before positively lit them up. It's why they have kept period features and tradition front of mind when creating the hotel's contemporary restaurant Abbey Row.

Time doesn't stand still in the kitchen, however. Menu highlights range from comforting classics (think memorable roasts and carefully crafted fish and chips) to inventive à la carte plates that satisfy the culinarily curious. Provenance is key, and the chefs prioritise using the very best,

whether that's produce from the local larder at Abbey House Manor Gardens or the freshest catch from Brixham Harbour.

In the bar, lounges and restaurant, luxury textures, a sophisticated palette and statement pieces combine to elegant effect without being overly formal. After all, The Old Bell Hotel chimes as the convivial heart of the community as much as the perfect place for a luxury escape.

Trencherman's tip

Those planning on exploring the Cotswolds should consider this a delightful base. Each room has its own personality and is decorated to exacting standards. Bath, Cirencester, Tetbury and an abundance of quintessentially English villages all lie within easy reach.

Chefs **Multiple** | 3-course dinner from **£80** | Seats **40** | Bedrooms **40** | Room rate from **£195**
oldbellhotel.co.uk | Abbey Row, Malmesbury, Wiltshire, SN16 0BW | **01666 822344**

111 Sam & Jak

Quality cooking with neighbourhood vibes

Though Edwards & Doggett could have been the monikers above the door, first names were a more apt reflection of the homely vibe chefs Sam and Jak sought to bring to Cirencester when they opened their restaurant in 2022.

This is a bistro that bridges cafe culture and destination dining. It's down to earth in a way that makes it feel like a relaxed neighbourhood fixture, yet the quality of the culinary offering is enough to lure the gastronomically minded from further afield.

An open kitchen, heritage palette of racing green and dryly humorous poster art provide personality, and the overall feel is modern vintage. Warm drop lighting draws the eye down to what really matters: what's on the table.

Thoughtful and original modern British dishes demonstrate flair in spades and are packed with taste and vibrancy. Pique your palate with Barnsley lamb served with french beans, fried polenta and anchoiade. Or plump for roasted jerusalem artichoke with wild mushrooms and truffle mash. Whatever's on the plate, it'll reflect Sam and Jak's commitment to ripe Cotswolds produce and their creative inspiration that day.

Trencherman's tip

Breakfast is an equally indulgent affair. Pair a flat white with a bulging bagel – the full sausage-bacon-egg trio or the halloumi and avocado with spicy honey and rocket are both a good shout.

Chef **Sam Edwards** | 3-course dinner from **£45** | Seats **50**
samandjak.co.uk | 2 Cricklade Street, Cirencester, Gloucestershire, GL7 1JH | **01285 704478**

Index

Huge thank you to the talented photographers whose images have been used throughout the guide: Matt Austin, JP Baudey, Luca Berardino, Mark Bolton, Kieran Brimson, Mark Cleghorn, Justin De Souza, Milly Fletcher, A Gilbert, Guy Harrop, Tommy Hatwell, Matthew Hawkey, Nick Hook, Matt Inwood, Marco Kesseler, Clare Kinchin, Alex Maguire, Alys Miller, Tom Leaper, Paul Massey, Tom Nicholson, Dan O'Regan, Ben Phillips, Andy Redgate, Adam Sargent, Nick Smith, Polly Stock, Stephen Studd, Jamie Thistlethwaite, Frankie Thomas, Jon Tonks, Two-D Photography, Angela Ward Brown, Dave Watts, WeTheFoodSnobs, Selena Young

Notes

For details of special dishes and drinks you've
experienced at Trencherman's restaurants

Notes

For details of special dishes and drinks you've experienced at Trencherman's restaurants

Notes

For details of special dishes and drinks you've experienced at Trencherman's restaurants

Notes

For details of special dishes and drinks you've
experienced at Trencherman's restaurants

edition
33

PARTNERS

CLASSIC
— FINE FOODS —

The CORNISH
FISHMONGER
From WING of St MAWES Ltd.

HALLGARTEN
& NOVUM WINES

HARVEY & BROCKLESS
the fine food c°

NAVAS
PREMIUM BOTANICAL MIXERS

EST · 1851
ST AUSTELL
BREWERY

St.Ewe
Delicious Free Range Eggs

TREVETHAN
SINCE 1929